Amsterdam and the Netherlands

The Most Comprehensive Travel
Guide to Experience the Best of
the City of Canals and the Hidden
Gems of Netherlands

Dream Scape Adventures

Table of Contents

Introduction

Welcome to the fascinating country of the Netherlands and Amsterdam! This travel manual is intended to assist you in organizing an enjoyable journey to this beautiful location. This book strives to provide you with the necessary knowledge and insider advice to maximize your trip, whether you're a seasoned traveler or a first-time visitor.

Learn about Amsterdam, a dynamic city renowned for its beautiful canals, historic landmarks, and bustling cultural scene. Get lost in the distinctive areas, including the famous Red Light District, the lovely Jordaan, and the energetic Leidseplein. Discover the city's renowned institutions, such as the Anne Frank House, Rijksmuseum, and Van Gogh Museum, where you can dig into art, history, and moving tales.

This itinerary also takes you on exhilarating side trips to the stunning Dutch countryside outside Amsterdam. Visit quaint cities with rich historical architecture and cultural legacy, such as Edam, Delft, and Haarlem. Visit the vivid bulb fields in the spring to witness the spectacular display of tulips in a kaleidoscope of hues. Immerse yourself in The Hague's political center or Rotterdam's cutting-edge architecture.

This book includes valuable information to make your vacation planning easier. Learn about Amsterdam's many lodging alternatives, from pricey hotels to free-of-charge hostels. Enjoy the rich culinary scene, where you may sample regional specialties and cuisines worldwide. Learn about Amsterdam's bike culture and take a local's perspective on the city. Find out about interesting retail possibilities and bring home genuine Dutch trinkets.

This resource also offers three-day vacation itineraries that may be used to see various parts of the Netherlands. You'll see the nation's varied landscapes, cultural sites, and hidden jewels, from the charming windmills at Zaanse Schans to the medieval city of Utrecht.

This guide also provides information on Dutch festivals and holidays, suggestions for books and movies to help you better understand Dutch culture, information on the local weather, and valuable Dutch words to help you communicate with people.

This guide will be your all-inclusive tool for making lifetime experiences in this exciting world region, whether you're drawn to Amsterdam's rich history, cultural legacy, or scenic surroundings. As you begin your wonderful tour, prepare to be enchanted by Amsterdam and the Netherlands' appeal.

Chapter 01
TRAVEL SMART

Traveling wise is crucial when arranging a vacation to guarantee a smooth and joyful experience. Making educated decisions and using resources efficiently are critical components of intelligent travel, which will help you get the most out of your time, money, and overall experience. You can streamline your vacation preparation and maximize your travel experience by implementing a few essential principles.

Conducting extensive research is a critical component of intelligent travel. Spend some time learning about your destination before setting off on your journey. Discover well-known sights, regional traditions, and cultural practices. Learn about the local transit systems, currencies, and languages. Making informed judgments about where to stay may be aided by researching lodging possibilities and reading reviews. Knowing what to do will enable you to make decisions that suit your tastes and avoid typical errors.

The creation of a thorough itinerary is another crucial aspect of wise travel. While being spontaneous may be fun, making the most of your time and money requires a general strategy. Determine the main attractions and experiences you want, and allot enough time for each. Consider the location's hours, the difficulty of getting there, and whether any reservations or tickets are necessary. But be sure to leave room for flexibility and relaxation so you may seize unanticipated chances or unwind and take in the atmosphere of your trip.

Being financially responsible is a crucial component of intelligent travel. Establish budgetary constraints and set aside money for lodging, travel, meals, activities, and souvenirs. Utilize possibilities to cut costs, such as scheduling travel and accommodation beforehand or during off-peak times. To sample the original flavors without breaking the wallet, research nearby eating alternatives and think about sampling local street food or inexpensive restaurants. Utilize discount websites, apps, and travel reward programs offering discounts on travel-related services.

Technology may be a valuable tool for intelligent travel in the digital era. Use websites and applications for trip planning to plan your schedule, monitor bookings, and access crucial information when offline. You may use navigational applications to identify the best routes to your destinations and traverse strange environments. Apps for money conversion and language translation can help you communicate with locals and keep track of exchange rates. Make digital copies of important papers like passports, visas, and travel insurance, and store them safely in the cloud for convenient access.

Being a wise traveler also means packing little. Examine the forecast for your location during the dates you want to travel and fill it appropriately. Consider layering alternatives for changing temps and choose versatile wardrobe pieces that may be combined and matched. Consider any limits airlines may impose while packing your essential personal belongings, prescriptions, and toiletries. Packing cubes and travel-sized containers can help you make the most of the space in your baggage and maintain organization. Don't forget to carry any chargers or adapters you might need for your electrical gadgets.

In conclusion, traveling wisely entails extensive research, planning a precise schedule, paying attention to your spending, employing technology, and packing effectively. Implementing these ideas into your trip preparation process may improve your travel experience, lessen stress, and make the most of your time and money. Remember that the objective is to balance rigidity and adaptability, leaving opportunities for spontaneity and unforeseen experiences. Travel safely!

Know Before You Go

Traveling is the most enjoyable activity, but if you don't do it properly, it may turn into a horrible experience. It must be well-researched and planned to be fun and memorable. Therefore, research your next journey before leaving your cozy cocoon and entering a foreign environment with a culture you've never encountered and strangers you've never met. The following list of things to know might help you fulfill your wanderlust more conveniently and hassle-free.

Things to keep in mind while picking a destination

1. Budget: Are you on a tight budget? You may enjoy several inexpensive overseas vacations.
2. Vacation duration: Consider the time you have available while planning your vacation.
3. Is the trip a romantic getaway? Family vacation? Business? Depending on why you are traveling, you should decide where to go.
4. You're traveling with Where you should go and shouldn't go significantly on who you're traveling with! You don't want to see your parents in Las Vegas, do you?

1. Do extensive research on your intended destination.

Priorities come first. Know where you're going. Find out information about:

1. Geography and climate: Going to Ladakh with severe asthma is probably not a brilliant idea.
2. Where to Eat: Research all the vegetarian restaurants in the city you're going to if you're one.
3. Which is the best mode of transportation: a plane, a train, or a car?
4. The best means of transportation in the city: Using the subway instead of paying for a private taxi will save you money.
5. Travel time and distance between various destinations or attractions: Using this information can help you schedule your touring each day.
6. Local laws, fundamental guidelines, and rules: Particularly for the UAE, Korea, and several other locations.
7. The current climate at the destination: It won't be fun to exit the airport wearing summer attire while it's pouring outside.
8. Basic terms in the destination's native tongue: Other than saying hello, goodbye, and thank you, helpful words in their language include "food," "water," "taxi," and "help."
9. Selecting the proper lodging: Before making a reservation, ensure you have clear access to hotel reviews and that your hotel is close to markets and public transportation.

10. Visa's unstated fees: Many nations that provide the Visa On Arrival service charge a price for it after you arrive in that nation. Ensure you know it well to avoid receiving a surprise at the airport.

2. Happy travel is a safe travel

While seeing other cultures and interacting with new people is excellent, don't sacrifice your health and well-being. Always keep your eyes and ears open. Before you travel, check out internet evaluations of the place, the hotel, the attractions, and pretty much everything.

1. Women's safety: Is it safe to take your girlfriends out clubbing at night in the location you're visiting?

2. Protect your possessions: Although Paris and Spain may be on your bucket list, theft, pickpocketing, and purse snatching are all too typical there, especially for visitors.

3. Keep everyone informed: Keep updating your status and checking in on social media, or at the very least, always let your friends and family know where you are and what the next step is! Stay in touch with your family at all times.

4. Make registering with your embassy a top priority. They can support you in case of emergency when traveling. Keep a list of Indian embassies' addresses and phone numbers in your pocket.

3. Make a travel plan

Research completed? Now, begin to prepare.

1. Please purchase your tickets after midnight, when they are most affordable.

2. Travel and airline websites may access your cookie data, which may analyze your browsing behavior (including which sites you regularly visit to check ticket costs and for which locations) and raise ticket prices. So, before purchasing tickets, delete your internet history.

3. Create a sensible itinerary: Just as few sightseeing alternatives as you can fit into each day. Avoid overbooking your schedule to avoid rushing between destinations and missing out on any of them.

4. Purchase advance tickets for attractions and events: Nothing beats making reservations in advance compared to standing in line afterward.

5. Get electronic maps and guidebooks for the location you're visiting ahead of time. Avoid relying just on physical ones.

6. Purchase customized travel packages: You may modify your itinerary to reflect your preferences and partake in activities you find appealing, all at relatively cheap costs.

4. Protect your travel documents

1. Make printouts of all of your travel papers, including your passport.

2. Leave a copy of your passport with a reliable person.

3. If you misplace your travel papers, scan them and keep them on your phone or laptop.

Send the scanned copies to your email address to access them if you misplace your phone.

5. Take care of your finances

Let's be honest. Nothing is worse than having to cope with financial problems overseas.

1. Research the nation you visit currency conversion rate and adjust your spending accordingly. Don't let this catch you off guard!
2. Call your credit card provider and let them know you intend to travel so they won't suspend your card when you purchase abroad.
3. Don't just rely on credit cards when you're abroad. Carry local currency, and avoid going to exchange bureaus for it. Instead, utilize the ATMs.

6. Reduce the amount of money spent on trips

Nobody enjoys taking a trip at the price of getting broke. Spend prudently and avoid wasting money.

1. Try to travel during off-peak times.
2. Use public transportation services for within-city travel.
3. Instead of feasting on upscale cuisine in restaurants, choose street food. That will, in any case, offer you a more incredible experience of the regional cuisine and culture.

What Essentials Pack For A Trip

Traveling is not only enjoyable, but it's also necessary for mental clarity when life starts to get stale. So, if you have also booked a trip, this piece is just for you. We'll teach you how to pack for a journey in this book. You must develop a list of everything you must bring on the vacation. You wouldn't want the fact that you forgot to bring the necessities to ruin your plans to wear a particular piece of clothing or pull off a specific hairstyle.

1. Packing list of clothing

1. Learn as much as you can about the local climate before your trip. Everything begins there.
2. Bring track trousers, shorts, and cozy T-shirts if you want to engage in many outdoor activities-shirts.
3. Start with the essentials, such as graphic T-shirts, intimates, pants, jeans, and shorts. Work your way through a dry run in your regular clothing.
4. Capsule clothing! Your strategy should be to mix and match. Pack judiciously so you may experiment with a minimal number of parts.
5. Bring adequate layers of clothing for your winter vacation. You can play around with everything in between.
6. Bring lightweight, quick-drying, and maintenance-free clothing if this is your first backpacking.

7. When traveling for a month across Europe, comfort is essential. Once more, pack for the weather. The same is true of journeys across North America.

8. One-piece outfits are a fantastic choice for a summer getaway. • Innerwear is an essential component of your packing because they take up little room in your bag and don't require a lot of clothing or style. Don't over or under-pack; just the right amount is plenty. Go over each item—tank tops, nude bras, sports bras, slips, camisoles, and panties—and carry the most easily.

2. Shoes

1. The majority of us make a mistake here. Don't go overboard with this. Carry one pair of shoes that you may use for strolling about, traveling, and anywhere else.

2. Carry a pair of party shoes that are practical and comfortable, such as a pair of black pumps or a pair of naked platforms, if you have a formal meal scheduled or plan to party a lot.

3. For a beach vacation, flip-flops or beach sandals are a given. But before leaving on a trip, make sure you've worn them for a while because brand-new flip-flops might be unpleasant.

4. Bring hiking boots, running or walking shoes, depending on your destination.

5. Generally speaking, closed-toed shoes are a good choice.

3. Cosmetics and Accessories

1. The correct accessories and cosmetics may completely change any look. Talk about stylish attire!
2. Do you still recall the concept of a capsule wardrobe? Accessories and makeup finish off that picture.
3. Any layers you can add or remove, such as scarves, shrugs, half-jackets, and sweaters, are a good choice.
4. Accessorize your purse with earrings, bold necklaces, finger rings, a side body bag, sunglasses, or anything else that will stand out and spice up your ensemble.
5. Bobby pins, clips, and hair ties are necessary for your hair.

4. Toiletries

You're good to go if you can get by with this trip component. Instead of buying full-sized bottles of goods, opt for travel-sized ones.

1. Before anything else, pack your necessities like facewash, shampoo, conditioner, a razor, toothpaste, sunscreen, deodorant, lotion, and perfume (8 oz or less).
2. Shampoo and soap are optional, as are hair styling supplies, toilet paper, and wet pipes, but hotels typically give some.

5. Electronics

Do you know the latest travel proverb? Bring your phone, charger, wallet, and other necessary equipment. The rest can be controlled.

1. A universal adaptor will be helpful if you are visiting another nation. You will need a voltage converter for your chargers and

heat styling products if the voltage capacity where you are visiting is different.

2. Don't forget to bring USB sticks, power banks, and memory cards.

6. Medicines and First Aid

1. If you are taking any medications, remember to keep them with you, even if you only take them rarely.

2. Band-aids, bandages, sanitizer, mosquito and insect repellents, and essential medications, including paracetamol, diarrhea medicine, painkillers, motion sickness tablets, and allergy medicines, are also necessary.

7. Travel paperwork

1. Prepare your travel paperwork, particularly if you're going overseas.

2. Keep your passport on you at all times.

3. Don't forget to bring your identity documentation, travel and medical insurance, and immunization records.

4. Create some contact papers for emergencies.

5. Any documents that need to be declared at the port of entry.

8. Travel Gear

1. If you're heading to the beach, a beach bag, hat, swimsuit, flip-flops, shades, flip-flops, sunglasses, and many sunscreens are essential. Plan your kit and do some research on the weather.

2. This includes camera bags, a handy backpack, a side body bag, shoes, water bottles, and other items that make your journey easier.

3. When traveling to a chilly location, you must pack items like leg warmers, raincoats, umbrellas, winter parkas, gloves, and socks.

4. If you want to hike, hiking boots and binoculars are a must.

5. You should rent extra-thick track trousers, jackets, or shoes if you're going skiing.

6. Pack everything you need for your trip in a bag. Such sturdy bags are even available for rental, so you can use them to transport your travel cushion and other belongings.

7. It would be easier to plan your needs if you have an itinerary of all the activities you want to accomplish. You can bring some supplies from home and pick up more when you get there.

9. Printout of the trip itinerary

1. Plan a thorough itinerary and decide which areas of the city you'll visit.

2. Keep an excel sheet updated, then print it. Organize information such as the closest bus or rail stops and their phone numbers, then pin it on your map.

3. Remember that you can only see so much of each location per visit. So, focus on a smaller subset of your interests by reading through some well-known how-to books and blogs and noting them.

4. Have some flexible soft spots in your daily short-shot strategy.

Finalize the checklists with the names of the hotels, phone numbers, and everything else that could be useful during your vacation. Make bookings in advance, pay online to avoid lines, and carry whatever you need to save money.

You can bring some food with you to eat on the journey. Don't forget to bring a diary and a pen so you may record your experiences and recollections. Carry your favorite books and earplugs to keep yourself amused and calm during the journey.

Travel Tips

We hope these excellent travel suggestions will help your upcoming vacation go much more efficiently, whether you travel for a week or a year.

1. Move Slowly

We usually provide the same advice when someone asks what our top travel tip is: calm down.

When you're on vacation, attempting to cram as many unique locations and experiences as possible is perfectly reasonable. Your time off from work is valuable, after all. But we assure you that taking time will give you more priceless experiences and memories.

The fact is that travel is taxing unless you're staying at an all-inclusive resort and don't intend to leave the grounds. Your senses continuously soak up your surroundings' fresh sounds, tastes, and scents.

If you're anything like us, you'll leave the hotel and spend the entire day walking around, visiting museums, scaling overlooks, and navigating tucked-away lanes. Even if you are on vacation, you are not relaxing.

Add to that the fact that if you're on a lengthy vacation, you also need to continuously consider how to go from one location to the next, where you're going to stay, how to obtain a visa while traveling, how to manage your funds, etc.

Simply slowing down is the most excellent way to avoid being utterly exhausted from all of this.

Spend extra time in each city you visit. Spend your mornings exploring and your afternoons relaxing in a cafe. Try not to cram too much into a short amount of time.

Longer stays also allow you to uncover hidden attractions, sample local cuisine, and perhaps even get better hotel rates.

We've attempted to accomplish it all in one week, spent seven months traveling throughout one nation, and everything in between. We can assure you that traveling slowly is more fulfilling and healthy for the soul.

2. When booking flights, think creatively

The airfare is the most costly component of your trip, depending on where you're going. The costs might even be excessive if you want to travel to a remote location.

We constantly strive to think creatively when looking for airfare because of this.

The initial step is to browse many websites for the most affordable choices. Wego, as one example, or straightforward web searches can help you save money on flights.

Instead of merely typing "Sydney to London," for instance, try ordering "Sydney to Singapore/Kuala Lumpur/Bangkok" or any other big hub, then ordering "Sydney to London" from there to see if there are any discounts on airlines that aren't affiliated with the same alliance.

Check out multi-trip tickets if you wish to have a stopover someplace else. As a result, we could spend three days in New York City for the exact cost of passing through.

3. Pick up a few words in the local tongue

Have you ever had a stranger approach you in your hometown and speak to you in a language you don't understand? The odds are slim or extremely infrequent if you reside in someplace like Australia or the United States.

It just wouldn't happen, and in specific locations, it may even be viewed as wholly undesirable.

Let's flip the coin: Have you ever visited a location where you are entirely unfamiliar with the native language? Where have you just approached a native and yelled something at them in English, hoping or expecting them to understand?

When speaking the local tongue, there seems to be a difference between saying it at home and traveling. But the truth is that learning a whole language for a destination you will visit for a few weeks is almost impossible.

However, that doesn't imply you shouldn't make an effort.

Our best travel advice is to pick up some of the fundamentals of the native language of the place you are going. To speak with a local in their language, try learning words and phrases like "hello," "thank you," "goodbye," "where is the bathroom?" and "how much."

This degree of courtesy will greatly enhance relationships between visitors and the local population. Ask a local to record those keywords in a notebook on your first day in a new country if you don't have time to learn from numerous applications before you leave home. Keep that notebook with you at all times.

4. Acquire travel protection

You cannot afford to go if you cannot afford travel insurance. It's a proverb spoken many times because it is wholly accurate.

Many people have chosen not to get travel insurance because they feel it is a waste of money, don't bring anything of value, or think that medical treatment everywhere they go is affordable.

Accidents happen, even if you don't think you'll become sick or aren't planning extreme activities.

5. Request Prices Before entering into any agreement

Never, and we mean never, enter a cab, book a tour, place an order at a nearby restaurant, or consent to anything involving money without first understanding the whole amount.

Unfortunately, there are a lot of places where dishonest locals may view visitors as walking money bags (particularly taxi drivers—let's not even start there). If you don't know how much anything is worth beforehand, they could think they can get away with charging you more when the deal is done.

Even if you know that they are trying to overcharge you, it may be challenging to negotiate a lesser price as you have already gotten your goods or service.

Therefore, our main advice when traveling is always to haggle and settle on a price in advance and make sure you work out all of the little issues beforehand (one-way or both ways, per person or overall, etc.).

6. Install a VPN

You need to understand how to secure sensitive data when browsing the web if you're anything like us and often connect to arbitrary wifi networks worldwide.

If you enter your bank login or credit card information on a network that has been compromised, you run the danger of having your accounts frozen. Hackers are becoming more intelligent and crafty and maybe watching online traffic on an open network.

We always utilize a VPN to establish a secure connection anytime we are dealing with money because of this.

Many social networking platforms and websites are blocked in some countries, but you can get past these limitations by using a VPN.

Additionally, this is incredibly helpful if you are attempting to utilize a geo-restricted website or may have different rates for customers purchasing goods outside of their native country.

(For instance, websites have attempted to charge us up to 25% extra for items when we try to purchase them from Australia. Change your location to the US, and you may buy the same thing for less!)

7. Obtain a credit or debit card with no foreign transaction fees

Did you know many banks will charge you a fee if you use an overseas ATM or transact in a different currency?

Typically, this consists of a currency conversion fee of 3% and a foreign transaction fee of $5. It might not seem like much, but if you're traveling for a while or often buying things in various currencies, this will mount up.

We constantly carry a variety of debit and credit cards with no fees for overseas transactions to minimize our unnecessary spending. Who wants to give banks more money at the end of the day?

You'll need to conduct your investigation to find out which banks in your nation provide these products.

8. Never exchange currency in your country of origin

About money, readers, friends, and family frequently ask us how to manage their access to cash when traveling. Just get your money there in the nation. We continually remind them.

The days of requiring traveler's checks or exchanging money in your native nation before departure are long gone.

Using these techniques will end up losing you money.

If you give airports and banks your business, you'll lose a lot of money in currency conversions because of their terrible exchange rates on foreign currency.

Instead, we advise delaying cash withdrawals until you are in the nation and using an ATM. Do you recall where you found that fantastic debit card with no foreign transaction fees? Yes, it will perform miracles in this situation.

Even if you don't have one of those beautiful cards, it is usually always more cost-effective to withdraw cash from an ATM than to exchange money at the bank or airport.

Most airports feature ATMs in the terminal for people who always want local cash when they land; while they could have higher ATM fees, you'll often obtain the most current exchange rate.

9. Keep many duplicates of all of your essential documents

You'd be shocked at how many locations want a copy of your passport, or in certain countries, like Iran, they may even ask to see your marriage license if you're sharing a room with your partner.

We advise having many photocopies of these vital documents in your bag so you may display them if necessary (without presenting the originals) rather than always carrying them.

Additionally, it's a good idea to take pictures of them and save them everywhere - send yourself an email with them, put them on Google Drive or Dropbox, and keep them in a convenient location on your phone.

10.   Always Be Charging (ABC)

This is especially crucial for individuals like us, who constantly use laptops, cameras, and phones. Charge them up!

Nothing is more annoying than discovering your phone or camera is dead after spending a whole day exploring.

Put whatever you can on a charge if you find yourself somewhere with a spare power outlet and some downtime since you never know when you'll have the opportunity to recharge your equipment.

A USB battery pack is another excellent product to charge your smaller devices all day without locating an outlet.

11.   Do Your Laundry to Save Money (and Time)

When you travel, take regular showers and carry enough clean clothing since the last thing you want to be is "that smelly backpacker."

We advise doing your laundry since you seldom have time to find a laundromat and wash your clothing while traveling

For years, we've always washed our clothing by hand (in sinks or the shower) and strung them on a clothesline without pegs in our room.

We do this for several reasons. It firstly helps you save money. While some hostels and hotels charge a few dollars for laundry or offer self-service laundry facilities, many demand exorbitant rates.

Another benefit is that it ensures that our clothing will not be lost. We can't remember how often we've gone to pick up the laundry only to discover that socks, underwear, or even t-shirts were missing.

12.   Get quick-drying clothing

This travel advice builds on the washing advice mentioned before. Always pack clothes that dry quickly. The logic very much speaks for itself.

As the name implies, quick-dry clothing is constructed of quick-drying materials. This is great if you frequently engage in outdoor activities where you can sweat or get wet. It's also great if you do your laundry quickly.

It must only be hung up for an hour or two in golden sunlight or fresh air to completely dry. Alternately, you may do what we do and put on a damp shirt, allowing the heat from your body to dry it.

13.   Bring earplugs

Even if you are the world's worst sleeper, packing earplugs might be the best (and least expensive) thing you ever do.

You never know when you'll find yourself attempting to get some shut-eye in a setting that is too noisy to fall asleep, whether from loud music on overnight buses or loud snorers in the tent next to you.

You don't need anything extravagant. All you need are essential foam earplugs from a hardware store.

14. Always have a water bottle with you

If you are concerned about the environment, bring a reusable aluminum water bottle on your trip.

Carry a metal bottle and fill it up when you're out and about in the town instead of constantly buying plastic water bottles.

You may drink tap water in most of Europe, North America, Australia, New Zealand, and some areas of South America, Asia, and Africa (but make sure to ask the natives first).

There is no justification for purchasing bottled water if you can travel to one of the fortunate nations where drinking water is available right from the faucet.

We advise purchasing the most significant water bottle you can find (5L, 10L, etc.) and filling your metal one before leaving for the day if you are in a location where you are unable to drink the tap water. You may reduce your consumption of plastic in this way.

Reverse osmosis units are located on every street in certain areas, like Thailand, and most hotels and pubs have water dispensers that will gladly fill your water bottle for a modest cost.

15. Get Your Phone a Local SIM Card

Nowadays, having internet connectivity when traveling is practically a need. There are several reasons to always have phone data available, from checking Google Maps to making last-minute hotel reservations to sharing your most excellent trip images on social media.

If your mobile phone plan doesn't include free worldwide data roaming, you'll probably incur exorbitant charges when you turn on your phone in a foreign country.

Even if your mobile phone operator offers a deal of $5–10 per day for international roaming, this will increase rapidly if you take a lengthy trip.

Our practice is to get a prepaid SIM card with data in each place we intend to visit for a week or more. It might surprise you how affordable this can be!

For this to function, your phone must be unlocked. Before purchasing a SIM card, research online to get the most excellent price.

Money management in traveling

One of the most frequent causes of stress for people is money. It doesn't matter how much money you have—something else always comes up. The price of meals, hotels, and sightseeing may rapidly increase while traveling. You may be considering how to better handle your finances while on the road so that you can unwind and take it easy.

Here are some pointers:

1. Don't bring all of your money along

Though it may seem paradoxical, heed our counsel. It's simple to spend money when you're lugging around a lot of it. Instead, make every effort to utilize your debit or credit card. Additionally, you may use ATMs to get cash when you need it. This will assist you in monitoring your expenditure and preventing overspending.

It's also a good idea to keep some cash at home in an emergency from a security standpoint. Choose the finest money transfer services if you need to send money to friends or relatives. You won't have all your eggs in one basket if your wallet is lost or stolen.

2. Create a budget

Figure out how much money you can afford to spend before you even begin packing for your vacation. Once you've decided on a sum, try to adhere to it. This is not to say that you can't indulge occasionally, but try to keep it to one or two major purchases rather than going overboard.

Even though it might seem apparent, it's crucial to sit down and determine how much cash you will require for your vacation. Ensure you have everything: food, housing, transportation, activities, and any keepsakes you want. When you have a specific amount in mind, you may save money every week or month until you have the required amount.

3. Be Aware Of Exchange Rates

Educating yourself about the exchange rate before traveling to a different country with a foreign currency is essential. You'll be aware of the value of your money in the local currency. This can aid in better budgeting and protect you from paying too much.

The most recent exchange rate is available online or at your neighborhood bank. Change money at a reputed location to receive the most effective exchange rate. You may use specific applications to track the currency rate and do conversions while on the road.

4. Use a credit card with travel rewards

It's a good idea to use a credit card that gives travel benefits if you intend to use it while traveling. Doing this allows you to accumulate points or miles for future trips. Remember to fully settle your account monthly to avoid accruing interest on your purchases.

A credit card with travel rewards might be a fantastic way to accumulate points or miles for use on future trips. Remember to fully settle your account monthly to avoid accruing interest on your purchases. Being mindful of your surroundings is crucial while taking money out of an ATM. Avoid utilizing machines at night and stick to those in well-lit locations. If feasible, try to locate an ATM within a bank or another establishment. This will assist you in avoiding fraud or theft.

5. Track Your Spending and Manage Your Money

It's simple to lose track of your travel expenses. When unfamiliar with the currency, everything appears to be more expensive. It's simple to spend money on pointless items. Please keep all of your receipts in one location to make it easier to keep track of your expenditures. You may also download budgeting software or create a spreadsheet to keep track of your spending.

You can prevent overspending and adhere to a budget by keeping track of your expenses. Choose the most effective approach among the several that exist.

6. Consistently Choose the Local Currency When Making a Credit Card Purchase

Choosing the local currency when paying usually is advisable if your credit card doesn't incur international transaction fees. You'll receive the finest exchange rate conceivable in this manner. To minimize costs, you might consider paying using your home currency if your card levies them.

Always use the local currency when using your credit card overseas to avoid paying international transaction fees. You might consider paying using your native money if your card has prices if you want to avoid them.

Using these suggestions, you may more effectively manage your finances while traveling and prevent overpaying. Keep in mind to plan and monitor your expenditures while on vacation. Planning beforehand allows you to enjoy yourself without exceeding your spending limit.

Transportation

Transportation when traveling may be considerably more straightforward than it used to be because of the abundance of alternatives in today's world, made possible by ride-sharing applications like Uber and Lyft.

No longer is it necessary to rely on maps or the word of locals. An app or navigation system can resolve many transportation concerns.

With so many choices, choosing which is ideal for you might be challenging. Where you're going might significantly impact the answer to that question; public transit might not be an option if you're going somewhere remote. While this might limit your options, deciding while planning a vacation overseas is still tricky.

Here are some possibilities for getting about when traveling, along with some advantages and disadvantages for each:

1. Apps for ride-sharing

Travelers are increasingly using ride-sharing applications, which may eventually replace other modes of transportation altogether. Tourists may travel directly to their destination and rarely need cash.

Most nations have shifted their taxi services to an app platform, even in countries where services like Lyft and Uber are unavailable. Find out which ride-sharing applications are most popular in each destination. Before you go, download the app to ensure you arrive at your destination.

The biggest concern with these applications is their safety. These worries will increase when traveling to a strange nation with a driver who might not know the language.

Safr is one of the ride-sharing applications that is designed exclusively for safe transportation. There are several suggested strategies to make sure a journey is risk-free when utilizing other applications.

2. Trains and Planes

Are you traveling throughout an area and stopping at several places? For a lengthy trip, driving might not be the best option.

Your timetable will probably affect which option is better.

Flights from one nation to another may be ideal for individuals with limited time and many sites to visit. As a result of the short distance you will be going, flights are quick and less expensive. The costs will be lower the more significant the city you're visiting. Travel to bigger European airports like Frankfurt, Paris, and London for a cheap holiday.

Train travel might be a more enjoyable option if you have a bit more time. Of course, taking the train takes longer than taking a plane, but it's also less expensive.

The train may take you on a brief tour of the nation. Train trips in countries like India, Japan, and South Africa are praised for their beauty. You can see snowy mountains, rainforests, and deserts from your cabin.

3. Using Public Transit

While traveling in Europe, public transit may be a fantastic, simple, and reliable choice.

Check to discover if the city you're visiting has a train, bus, or other general public transit system. These choices may not be available everywhere, especially when visiting a remote location.

Before traveling to the nation, find out how to get passes or tickets for the public transit system. Traveling without a ticket carries significant repercussions in several countries.

Additionally, it's crucial always to watch your possessions if you're traveling by public transit. Always carry your bag close to your body or keep it in front of you if you're traveling with a bag or handbag. Keep valuables out of your pockets, where pickpockets, such as your wallet or passport, may quickly get them.

4. Renting a car

The best solution may also be the most expensive one.

Anyone who requires flexibility in their travel arrangements may find that renting a car is the best solution. The rental may be the best option if you wish to travel carefree or have the flexibility to make impromptu plans.

Remember that every nation will have different driving rules. To avoid driving on the wrong side of the road if you hire a car, familiarize yourself with these regulations. A foreign driver's license or supplementary insurance may also be required.

Additionally, several nations only provide manual transmissions in their automobiles instead of automatic ones.

Chapter 02
Amsterdam

Amsterdam's dynamic and alluring city, the Netherlands' capital, enchants tourists worldwide. Amsterdam provides a distinctive fusion of rich cultural legacy and contemporary metropolitan living. It is known for its gorgeous canals, ancient buildings, and open-minded culture.

Amsterdam is known as the "Venice of the North" because of its intricate network of canals, which is one of its distinguishing characteristics. Exploring these canals bordered by lovely homes, on foot, by bike, or during a leisurely boat excursion is preferable. The Grachtengordel, a 17th-century canal ring region of the city, is a UNESCO World Heritage site and a reminder of Amsterdam's lengthy past.

Amsterdam has several top-notch museums, cultural organizations, and picturesque canals. The Van Gogh Museum displays the most exmost extensive collection of Vincent van Gogh's artwork, while the Rijksmuseum displays Dutch art and history, including works by Rembrandt and Vermeer. The Stedelijk Museum showcases modern and contemporary art, while the Anne Frank House offers a moving look into the famed diarist's life during the Holocaust.

Each of Amsterdam's different districts has its unique personality and allure. The Jordaan area is a favorite for locals and tourists with its little alleys, chic shops, and inviting cafés. While the fashionable Oud-West area provides a mix of boutique stores, hipster cafés, and green spaces like Vondelpark, the De Pijp sector is famed for its lively Albert Cuyp Market.

Amsterdam is praised for its modern outlook and open mentality. The city's varied population and liberal politics prove its long tolerance history. Despite its reputation, Amsterdam's famed Red Light District symbolizes the city's tolerance and openness to all lifestyles. The town also holds a lot of festivals and events all year long that highlight the diversity of cultures and the arts.

With a vast network of bike lanes and rental choices accessible for tourists, bicycles are an essential element of Amsterdam's culture. Getting about the city on two wheels is a common and environmentally beneficial method that gives you a distinctive viewpoint and lets you fit in with the locals.

Amsterdam is well-known not just for its cultural attractions but also for its exciting nightlife. The city has a booming bar and club culture, with many diverse venues that appeal to various tastes. Everyone looking for amusement after dark will find it here, from classic Dutch "brown cafes" to hip cocktail bars and underground clubs.

Overall, Amsterdam is a city that skillfully blends its rich past with a future-focused outlook. Travelers looking for a distinctive and unforgettable experience will find it an enticing destination thanks to its picturesque canals, top-notch museums, lively districts, and open-minded attitude.

Sights in Amsterdam

Amsterdam is teeming with fascinating attractions that provide an insight into its illustrious past, diverse culture, and stunning architecture. Here are a few of Amsterdam's must-see attractions:

1. The Anne Frank House is a museum housed in the hiding place that Anne Frank and her family used to survive World War II. It offers a stirring and compelling glimpse into Anne's life and the atrocities of the Holocaust.

2. The Rijksmuseum: The Rijksmuseum is the most significant art museum in the Netherlands and is home to a sizable collection of Dutch artwork and historical artifacts. It displays works of art by well-known artists, including Rembrandt, Vermeer, and Van Gogh.

3. Van Gogh Museum: This museum, which is devoted to the life and works of Vincent van Gogh, houses the most extensive collection of his paintings and sketches in existence. Visitors may learn more about the artist's journey and his artistic brilliance.

4. The Jordaan: This scenic district is well-known for its winding canals, lovely canal houses, and old structures. With its boutique stores, art galleries, quaint cafés, and bustling markets, it provides a beautiful environment.

5. The Royal Palace, the National Monument, and the Nieuwe Kerk (New Church) are significant structures surrounding the busy Dam Square in the center of Amsterdam. It is a bustling gathering spot and a fantastic place to begin exploring the city.

6. Vondelpark: Vondelpark, the most well-known park in Amsterdam, offers a haven of greenery in the city's heart. It's ideal for strolls, picnics, cycling, or just unwinding in the splendor of nature.

7. The Heineken Experience: The Heineken Experience, an interactive museum housed in the former Heineken plant, is a must-see for beer fans. It provides a thorough tour of the brewing process and the background of this well-known Dutch beer brand.

8. The Red Light District: Though debatable, Amsterdam's Red Light District is unquestionably distinctive. The city's openness to the sex trade is evident in its winding lanes and lit windows.

9. NEMO scientific Museum: NEMO is a hands-on science museum with interactive displays, experiments, and workshops, making it the perfect location for families and curious minds. It is shaped like a vast green ship.

These are just a handful of the countless sites that Amsterdam has to offer. The city's beauty comes in its ability to seamlessly combine historical significance with cutting-edge attractions, providing tourists with a remarkable experience.

Amsterdam City Walk

Walking about Amsterdam is a great way to experience the city's distinct vibe and uncover its hidden jewels. Here is a recommended walking path that visits some of the main attractions:

1. Dam Square: Begin your city stroll at Amsterdam's busy center, Dam Square. Admire the magnificent Nieuwe Kerk (New Church), the National Monument, and the Royal Palace surrounding the plaza.

2. Kalverstraat: From Dam Square, proceed in the direction of Kalverstraat, one of the leading retail streets in Amsterdam. Explore this bustling pedestrian strip, surrounded by various stores, boutiques, and restaurants.

3. The Jordaan: Head west in the direction of the lovely Jordaan area. Discover its charming streets, lined with gorgeous canal homes, art galleries, boutique stores, and inviting cafés. The renowned Nine Streets (De Negen Straatjes), a series of eerie alleyways bursting with distinctive stores and restaurants, should not be missed.

4. Visit the Anne Frank House on Prinsengracht while you are in the Jordaan. This museum provides a profoundly touching and instructive experience by guiding visitors through the location of Anne Frank's World War II hiding spot.

5. Westerkerk and Homomonument: The Westerkerk is a magnificent Protestant church from the 17th century close to the

Anne Frank House. Atop its tower, you may get a bird's-eye perspective of the city. The Homomonument, a memorial to LGBTQ+ rights and a significant marker of tolerance in Amsterdam stands immediately next to the cathedral.

6. Museumplein: Travel south to reach Museumplein, a bustling area with some of Amsterdam's best museums. Visit the Van Gogh Museum to explore the artist's creations, the Rijksmuseum to view Dutch treasures, or the Stedelijk Museum to view modern and contemporary art.

7. Vondelpark: The largest city park in Amsterdam, Vondelpark, is a tranquil place to end your city stroll. To relax, take in the scenery, take a walk, hire a bike, or pick a sunny area. You could be fortunate to witness a show in the park's outdoor theater.

Of course, you can alter this itinerary to suit your preferences and the available time or visit additional areas and attractions. Amsterdam is a city that invites investigation, and as you meander through its streets, you're sure to find beautiful discoveries.

Centrum district

The historic city core and beating center of Amsterdam is the Centrum neighborhood. It is a bustling, energetic region with unique landmarks, lovely canals, quaint streets, and a blend of old and contemporary buildings. The following are some of the district's highlights:

1. Dam Square: Located in the center of Centrum, Dam Square is an active meeting place and a significant historical landmark. The National Monument, the Nieuwe Kerk, and the Royal Palace are nearby.

2. The Canal Belt: The renowned canal belt of Amsterdam, a UNESCO World Heritage site, is located in the Centrum neighborhood. Herengracht, Keizersgracht, and Prinsengracht, the city's three principal canals, create concentric rings around the city's core and are flanked with lovely canal residences, endearing bridges, and houseboats.

3. The Anne Frank House: The Anne Frank House is a must-see sight and is located on the Prinsengracht waterway. It is now a museum where visitors may learn about Anne Frank's life and the Holocaust. This is the natural home that Anne Frank and her family fled to during World War II.

4. The Jordaan: The Jordaan area, which lies next to the canal belt, is renowned for its charming streets, art galleries, inviting cafés, and boutique stores. It has a pleasant vibe and is a beautiful location for exploring and aimless wandering.

5. De Wallen (Red Light District): The Red Light District is more than simply its notoriety, despite being known for its red-lit windows. It offers a distinctive ambiance, with winding alleyways, old buildings, various pubs, eateries, and places to go for adult

entertainment. The Oude Kerk, Amsterdam's oldest structure, is also located there.

6. Nieuwmarkt: This bustling square can be found in the Centrum neighborhood's eastern section. The Waag, a medieval gatehouse that today doubles as a café and a museum, is located there, and ancient structures, cafes, and eateries flank it.

7. Damrak and Rokin: These vibrant streets link Centraal Station to Dam Square. They have a bustling environment with street entertainers and different attractions bordered by stores, restaurants, and hotels.

8. Rembrandtplein: This lively plaza bears the well-known Dutch painter's name, Rembrandt van Rijn's name. It is a famous area for nightlife, and many pubs, clubs, and eateries exist. Rembrandt's figure dominates the site, which is encircled by old structures.

9. Flower Market: Amsterdam's floating flower market, situated on the Singel canal, is a vibrant and aromatic sight. It is a well-liked location for locals and tourists since it offers many flowers, bulbs, and gifts.

10. The Royal Palace: The Royal Palace (Koninklijk Paleis), a stately structure first constructed as a municipal hall in the 17th century, is located on Dam Square. The public can visit one of the three official houses of the Dutch royal family at this time.

The Centrum neighborhood of Amsterdam is like entering a living museum with its fascinating history, stunning architecture, and lively environment. It is a location where the ancient and the new coexist, and every turn offers something delightful.

Red Light District

Amsterdam's Red Light District is a well-known and distinctive location that has drawn interest worldwide. Here are some essential details to comprehend regarding the Red Light District:

1. Location: The Red Light District, commonly known as "De Wallen," is located within the Centrum neighborhood in the historic city center of Amsterdam. With Oudezijds Voorburgwal as its main thoroughfare, it is surrounded by canals.

2. Red-Lit Windows: The neighborhood is well-known for its red-lit windows, which serve as billboards for sex workers. The dimly lit windows that line the winding streets and lanes provide a distinctive ambiance. Note that the Red Light District is a recognized area for this industry and that sex work is legal and regulated in the Netherlands.

3. History: Sailors and traders first came to the Red Light District in the 14th century, and the region has a rich history. Over time, it developed into a center for entertainment, with theaters, clubs, brothels, and a prostitution hotspot.

4. Oude Kerk (Old Church): Situated in the Red Light District, the Oude Kerk is the oldest structure in Amsterdam. This ancient church is worth visiting for its lovely interior and peaceful

ambiance since it offers a historical and architectural contrast to the neighborhood.

5. The Red Light District's tiny alleyways and canals contribute to its charm. The neighborhood's lovely canals, endearing bridges, and eerie passageways provide an exciting setting for exploring.

6. Coffeeshops and Cafés: Besides the red-lit windows, there are many coffee shops in the Red Light District where cannabis products are available for sale and use. These places provide a laid-back atmosphere and adhere to the Netherlands' tolerance drug policy.

7. Nightlife & Entertainment: The Red Light District comes alive at night with various nightlife alternatives. It draws residents and visitors looking for nightlife with multiple bars, clubs, theaters, and adult entertainment establishments.

8. Cultural and Historical value: The Red Light District has cultural and historical significance and is known for its adult entertainment business. The region has seen urban growth, architectural modifications, and social changes throughout the years, making it an exciting location to investigate from a historical and sociological standpoint.

9. Respect and Etiquette: When visiting the Red Light District, visitors should show courtesy to the sex workers and the locals. Disturbing the workers' jobs or acting rudely or disruptively is highly forbidden. Remembering that a district is a place of

employment for the parties concerned is crucial. Therefore respect must be shown.

10. Moving Beyond Stereotypes: While the Red Light District is well-known for its adult entertainment business, Amsterdam is a bustling city with much more to offer. The city's vast and varied offers may be better understood by venturing outside the area and investigating different neighborhoods, cultural centers, and attractions.

It's critical to approach the Red Light District with an open mind and an eagerness to comprehend its intricate dynamics. While it might not be to everyone's taste, it contributes to Amsterdam's cultural scene in a distinctive and essential historical way.

Nieuwmarkt

The Centrum neighborhood's Nieuwmarkt is a bustling area in the eastern section of Amsterdam's old city center. The following are some crucial details regarding Nieuwmarkt:

1. Geographic location: Nieuwmarkt is bounded by Zeedijk, Kloveniersburgwal, Geldersekade, and Sint Antoniesbreestraat and is close to the Oude Kerk (Old Church).

2. Historical Importance: Nieuwmarkt has a lengthy past that dates to the 17th century when it was used as a marketplace. It served as a protective wall and was formerly an integral feature of the city's defenses. The region still has some of the medieval city walls visible today.

3. Market Square: Every Saturday, The lively market is known as Nieuwmarkt Square. Fresh fruit, flowers, apparel, and food stalls selling delectable treats from many cuisines are among the many available products.

4. De Waag: De Waag, a medieval gatehouse that formerly functioned as a city gate and a component of the city walls, is one of the famous structures on Nieuwmarkt Square. Today, it is a historic structure that houses a museum and a café. De Waag is an eye-catching building and a well-known representation of Amsterdam's history.

5. Cafés and Restaurants: The area around Nieuwmarkt is filled with cafes, pubs, and eateries that provide a wide variety of food. Locals and tourists alike use this popular location to unwind with a meal or drink and take in the lively ambiance of the plaza.

6. Chinese Quarter: Amsterdam's Chinatown is located in the vicinity of Nieuwmarkt. One of the streets near Nieuwmarkt, Zeedijk, is packed with Chinese eateries, stores, and cultural centers. It's a beautiful location to discover and sample real Chinese food.

7. Oude Kerk (Old Church): The Oude Kerk, the oldest structure in Amsterdam, is close by and well worth a visit. It offers a calm and historic ambiance compared to the busy Nieuwmarkt Square.

8. Nightlife: Nieuwmarkt and its streets come alive at night with a thriving nightlife. Visitors may enjoy live music, drinking, and dancing at several bars and clubs the night away.

9. Proximity to other attractions: The Red Light District, the Amsterdam Museum, the Rembrandt House Museum, and the Waterlooplein flea market are all within easy walking distance of Nieuwmarkt. Being in the city's center, it's an ideal place to start your explorations.

Nieuwmarkt offers a distinctive fusion of entertainment, culture, and history. It is a lively and engaging location to explore in Amsterdam due to its bustling market, ancient structures, and diversified food scene.

Plantage

East of the city's core is where Amsterdam's Plantage area is situated. Here are some of the neighborhood's most notable characteristics and draws:

1. The oldest zoo in the Netherlands, Artis, is located in Plantage. Lions, elephants, giraffes, penguins, and a wide variety of other creatures are among the intriguing species that may be seen at Artis Royal Zoo. The zoo's amenities include a planetarium, an aquarium, and lovely botanical gardens.

2. Hortus Botanicus: One of the world's oldest botanical gardens, Hortus Botanicus is located next to Artis. Various plants, including rare and exotic species, are kept there. Visitors may learn about plant protection, meander through serene gardens, and discover multiple temperature zones.

3. Micropia: Right adjacent to Artis and the Hortus Botanicus is the unusual museum known as Micropia. It highlights the unseen life forms around us by concentrating on the intriguing world of microorganisms. Visitors to the exhibitions can learn more about the function of bacteria in ecological and human systems.

4. Wertheimpark: Abraham Carel Wertheim is honored by Plantage's attractive Wertheimpark, a peaceful park. The park offers a tranquil getaway in the middle of the city with lovely green areas, a pond, and sculptures.

5. Portuguese Synagogue: The Portuguese Synagogue is a notable landmark in the area and is part of Plantage's rich historical Jewish legacy. One of the most prominent synagogues in the world, this magnificent structure from the 17th century is still utilized for religious services and other gatherings.

6. Verzetsmuseum: The Dutch Resistance Museum offers information on the experiences of Dutch people during World War II. The museum recounts the resistance actions against the Nazi occupation through its exhibitions, relics, and personal accounts.

7. Tropenmuseum: The Tropenmuseum provides a distinctive viewpoint on civilizations and ethnography worldwide. It explores the history, art, and customs of cultures worldwide by showcasing various exhibitions and relics from multiple locales.

8. Plantage Doklaan: This charming canal-lined street in the area is well-known for its exquisite 19th-century structures. It offers a relaxing environment for a stroll and provides a view of Amsterdam's architectural history.

9. Café-Restaurant De Plantage: Plantage offers a choice of food alternatives in addition to its cultural attractions. In a former greenhouse, Café-Restaurant De Plantage is a well-liked destination for breakfast, lunch, and supper. It offers a chic atmosphere and a Dutch and foreign cuisine menu.

Amsterdam's Plantage area blends the city's natural beauty with cultural organizations and historic sites. While providing a variety of exciting events for guests to enjoy, it offers a refreshing break from the city core.

Amsterdam-Oost

On the eastern side of the city, in a district known as Amsterdam-Oost or Amsterdam East, is a vibrant and varied community. The following are some of Amsterdam-Oost's main characteristics and draws:

1. Oosterpark: A well-liked park in Amsterdam-Oost, Oosterpark provides a tranquil location for leisure, picnics, and outdoor sports. Throughout the year, the park also organizes several festivals and events.

2. Dappermarkt: This bustling street market has been running since the late 19th century and is situated in the center of Amsterdam-

Oost. Fresh vegetables, apparel, flowers, and exotic cuisine are just a few products it sells.

3. Tropenmuseum: The Tropenmuseum, which was previously mentioned, is a renowned cultural facility in Amsterdam-Oost. Its extensive collection of artifacts, exhibitions, and interactive displays illustrate the various cultures and histories of the tropics.

4. Javastraat: The center of Amsterdam-Oost is located on this bustling street. It is renowned for its cosmopolitan ambiance, with a wide variety of stores, eateries, pubs, and cafés serving food worldwide.

5. Oostelijk Havengebied: The Oostelijk Havengebied, often known as Eastern Docklands, is a former industrial region now home to a contemporary residential and business zone in Amsterdam-Oost. It has cutting-edge architecture, waterfront walkways, and cultural hubs like the renowned music theater Muziekgebouw aan 't IJ.

6. Flevopark: On the northeastern outskirts of Amsterdam-Oost, a sizable park called Flevopark. It has many open green spaces, wooded areas, walking trails, and even a little beach at Nieuwe Diep lake. It's the ideal location for outdoor pursuits, picnics, or just taking in nature.

7. Oostpoort: In Amsterdam-Oost, Oostpoort is a bustling, recently constructed neighborhood. It blends residential structures with

shops, eateries, and cafés. The old city gate, one of the district's preserved historical features, uniquely appeals to the area.

8. OLVG Hospital: The OLVG Hospital (Onze Lieve Vrouwe Gasthuis), one of the city's principal medical institutions, is in Amsterdam-Oost. It offers medical services to the neighborhood and beyond.

9. Flevoparkbad: Flevopark is home to the well-liked public swimming pool known as Flevoparkbad. During the warmer months, it has outdoor swimming pools where visitors may swim, sunbathe, and engage in other activities.

10. Muiderpoort Station: Located in Amsterdam-Oost, Muiderpoort is a historic train station. It is a transportation center and an architectural icon, distinguished by its recognizable clock tower and elaborate exterior.

Amsterdam-Oost is a bustling area that mixes diverse cultures, open spaces, and contemporary construction. It provides a variety of attractions, such as parks, marketplaces, cultural centers, and a genuine metropolitan setting. Amsterdam-Oost has a lot to offer, whether you want to discover local markets, take in the beauty of nature, or experience a diverse range of cultures.

Oosterdok

The neighborhood of Oosterdok in Amsterdam is well-known for its bustling waterfront and selection of leisure facilities. The following are some of Oosterdok's main attributes and draws:

1. Central Station: Oosterdok is a gateway to the city, immediately east of Amsterdam's Central Station. Beautiful views of the station's beautiful architecture and the busy ambiance of the transit hub are available in the neighborhood.

2. NEMO Science Museum: The NEMO Science Museum is one of Oosterdok's most recognizable sights. NEMO offers interactive exhibits and hands-on activities that make science and technology approachable and entertaining for visitors of all ages. It is housed in a distinctive green ship-shaped structure.

3. National nautical Museum (Het Scheepvaartmuseum): The National Maritime Museum is a must-see destination for marine enthusiasts and is located on the eastern side of Oosterdok. It highlights the Netherlands ' rich nautical past through exhibits, relics, engaging displays, and even the chance to board a model Dutch East India Company ship.

4. Public Library (Openbare Bibliotheek Amsterdam): The Public Library's magnificent, contemporary structure dominates the skyline of Oosterdok. In addition to being a library, it has meeting rooms, exhibition spaces, and a rooftop café with sweeping views of Amsterdam.

5. OBA Oosterdok: OBA Oosterdok, a branch of the Public Library, is Amsterdam's most extensive public library. It provides a sizable library, online resources, and a variety of cultural activities, including talks, seminars, and exhibitions.

6. Passenger Terminal Amsterdam: The Passenger Terminal Amsterdam is a cruise terminal along Oosterdok's waterfront. Numerous cruise ships are welcomed there, adding to the lively atmosphere.

7. Oosterdokseiland: Located in Oosterdok, Oosterdokseiland is a freshly constructed island with contemporary homes, businesses, and hotels. It offers a variety of residential and business areas, as well as eateries, cafés, and retail establishments.

8. Oosterdokskade: This waterfront walkway runs the length of Oosterdok on its eastern side. It provides beautiful views of the town, boats, and the ocean. The promenade is a well-liked location for a leisurely bike ride or walk.

9. Bars and Restaurants: Oosterdok has many bars and restaurants, from little cafés to elegant dining facilities. A variety of cuisines, including both foreign and traditional Dutch fare, are available for visitors to sample.

Oosterdok is a bright and active neighborhood of Amsterdam because it provides a variety of cultural, educational, and recreational activities. Oosterdok offers a stimulating backdrop for learning about the greatest of Amsterdam's culture and history, whether your interests are museums, the waterfront, or the city's architectural masterpieces.

Western Islands

The Westelijke Eilanden, sometimes referred to as the Western Islands, are a collection of islands situated west of Amsterdam, Netherlands. The Western Islands' main characteristics and draws are as follows:

1. Prinseneiland: Of all the Western Islands, Prinseneiland is the most significant and best-known island. It has gorgeous residences, quaint bridges, and scenic lanes surrounded by old warehouses. The ambiance of the isle is evocative of Amsterdam's earlier seafaring days.

2. Bickerseiland: Another island in the Western Islands group is called Bickerseiland. It is renowned for its picturesque canals, historic structures, and peaceful ambiance. It provides a tranquil haven away from the busy city hub.

3. Realengracht: The Realengracht is the principal canal linking Prinseneiland and Bickerseiland in the Western Islands. It enhances the area's appeal by providing stunning vistas and a tranquil atmosphere.

4. Historical Architecture: The Western Islands are home to many historically significant structures, including beautifully maintained homes and warehouses. These buildings offer a look into Amsterdam's industrial and marine past.

5. Westerdok: The Western Islands are next to a little harbor called Westerdok. It is a well-liked location for boating lovers, providing

moorings for boats and yachts. The neighborhood offers a relaxing seaside environment for strolls and beautiful vistas.

6. Westerdokseiland: Situated close to the Western Islands, Westerdokseiland is a modern development. It has parks, seafront promenades, and contemporary housing structures. The region mixes a hint of modern metropolitan style with the rustic allure of the Western Islands.

7. Cafe-Restaurant Piet de Gruyter: This well-known restaurant in Prinseneiland is famous for its warm and inviting ambiance. It is renowned for its delectable fare, refreshing beverages, and kind service.

8. Exploring by bicycle or on foot is a great way to experience the Western Islands. It is a friendly and handy area to roam about and find hidden jewels because of the islands' small size and lovely streets.

The Western Islands in Amsterdam provide a singular experience by giving visitors a look into the city's nautical heritage while preserving a quaint and tranquil ambiance. It's a location where guests can escape the bustle of the city center and take in the picturesque splendor of old buildings, canals, and a laid-back atmosphere.

Amsterdam-Noord

Across the IJ River from the city center lies the dynamic and quickly developing district known as Amsterdam-Noord, or North Amsterdam.

The following are some of Amsterdam Noord's main characteristics and draws:

1. Eye Film Institute: Located on the IJ River's banks, the Eye Film Institute is a distinctive architectural icon. It is a well-known cultural center devoted to film and cinema, complete with a museum, movie theaters, exhibition spaces, and a rooftop terrace with breathtaking city views.

2. NDSM Wharf: Formerly a shipyard, NDSM Wharf has become a hub for the arts and culture. It has galleries, cafés, restaurants, and artist studios and regularly holds events, festivals, and exhibitions. It serves as a center for modern design, art, and urban culture.

3. A'DAM Tower: Located in Amsterdam-Noord, A'DAM Tower is a well-known high-rise structure with several attractions. Visitors may experience the exhilarating "Over the Edge" swing that hangs over the side of the skyscraper, dine at the rotating restaurant, or take in panoramic views of the city from the observation deck.

4. Tolhuistuin: Housed in a former Shell office building, Tolhuistuin is a cultural establishment. It holds various events, including plays, concerts, and art shows. The location also has a lovely waterfront patio and a café-restaurant.

5. Pllek: Situated on Amsterdam-Noord's waterfront, Pllek is a well-liked beach-style eatery and gathering place for the arts. It provides a chill environment, live music, organic food, and

breathtaking cityscape views. The distinctive shipping container architecture of Pllek is well known.

6. Noorderlicht Café: Located on the NDSM Wharf in a building that resembles a greenhouse, Noorderlicht Café is a laid-back café and cultural hub. It holds exhibits, DJ evenings, and live music events. The outside patio offers a pleasant atmosphere to partake in food and beverages.

7. Vliegenbos: Located in Amsterdam-Noord, Vliegenbos is the oldest urban forest in the city and a tranquil green haven. It has a campsite, picnic areas, and walking and cycling pathways. It's the perfect spot to escape the city and reconnect with nature.

8. EYE Filmmuseum: Besides the Eye Film Institute already stated, the EYE Filmmuseum's collection center is in Amsterdam-Noord. This cutting-edge center is devoted to preserving, restoring, and studying historical film.

9. Ferries to Central Station: A free ferry service connects Amsterdam-Noord to the city center. These boats offer a fun and beautiful method to go between the two locations, leaving from behind Amsterdam Central Station.

A vibrant fusion of art, culture, urban growth, and scenic beauty can be found in Amsterdam-Noord. It has experienced tremendous alteration recently and is now a well-liked tourist attraction. Amsterdam-Noord offers a unique and rewarding experience in the city with its cutting-edge architecture, creative spaces, waterfront vistas, and cultural attractions.

Western Canal Ring

A historic area of Amsterdam known for its attractive canals, quaint alleyways, and exquisite canal homes is known as the Western Canal Ring. It is a piece of the more excellent Canal Belt, a concentric ring of canals surrounding the city center and classified by UNESCO. Here are some of the Western Canal Ring's main attributes and draws:

1. Prinsengracht: The Western Canal Ring's principal canal, Prinsengracht, is flanked by opulent canal mansions and recognizable monuments. It offers picturesque vistas and photo ops and is named for the Prince of Orange.

2. Keizersgracht: Also referred to as the Emperor's Canal, Keizersgracht is a significant canal in the Western Canal Ring. It bears the name Maximilian I of the Holy Roman Empire and is renowned for its opulent canal mansions and banks adorned with trees.

3. Herengracht: Also known as the Gentlemen's Canal, Herengracht is one of Amsterdam's most renowned and historic waterways. It has grand mansions, historical structures, and the famous "Golden Bend," an area renowned for its affluent homes.

4. Anne Frank House: The Anne Frank House, situated on Prinsengracht, is an important historical location where Anne Frank and her family fled the Nazis during World War II. It

functions as a museum today, keeping Anne Frank's legacy alive and shedding light on the Holocaust.

5. Westerkerk: A well-known landmark on the Western Canal Ring is the Westerkerk, also known as the West Church. One of the highest in Amsterdam, its recognizable tower provides sweeping city vistas. Rembrandt, a well-known Dutch painter, is also buried in the cathedral.

6. Noordermarkt is a bustling square on the Western Canal Ring that features a well-liked farmers market on Saturdays and a flea market on Mondays. It features a variety of vendors offering organic, vintage, and antique things as well as fresh food.

7. Jordaan: The Western Canal Ring neighborhood of Jordaan is a historic district renowned for its quaint alleys, boutique stores, art galleries, and pleasant cafés. It is a popular location for locals and tourists to explore and take in the area's bohemian vibe.

8. The Nine Streets (De Negen Straatjes): The Nine Streets are charming streets connecting the principal canals inside the Western Canal Ring. It is a shopping and dining destination thanks to its renowned boutique shops, independent retailers, vintage shops, and fashionable cafes.

9. Houseboat Museum: This one-of-a-kind site in the Western Canal Ring allows visitors to board a typical Dutch houseboat and learn about the culture and way of life of people who live on boats.

The Western Canal Ring, with its opulent canal residences, historic sites, and lively environment, epitomizes the characteristic beauty of Amsterdam's canal system. Visitors may immerse themselves in the city's rich history, architectural legacy, and quaint atmosphere by exploring this neighborhood. The Western Canal Ring offers a typical Amsterdam experience, whether you meander along the canals, visit museums, or indulge in shopping and dining.

Eastern Canal Ring

Part of Amsterdam's historic Canal Belt, which UNESCO classifies, is the Eastern Canal Ring. It lies east of the city center and offers a variety of cultural and architectural attractions in addition to lovely canals and attractive canal residences. The Eastern Canal Ring's main characteristics and draws are listed below:

1. Hermitage Amsterdam: The Hermitage Amsterdam is a branch of the famed Hermitage Museum in St. Petersburg, Russia, situated on the banks of the Amstel River. It holds revolving exhibits that feature works of art and artifacts from the extensive museum collection.

2. Skinny Bridge (Magere Brug): The Skinny Bridge spans the Amstel River charmingly and recognizably. One of Amsterdam's most well-known bridges, it offers breathtaking vistas, especially at night when lit.

3. The Amstelkerk is a lovely 17th-century church transformed into a cultural center. It sponsors performances, exhibits, and other cultural occasions that merge classical and modern art genres.

4. Royal Theater Carré: Situated on the Amstel River, the Royal Theater Carré is a historic theater. It is well-known for its elaborate exterior and presents a variety of acts, including theater, ballet, concerts, and comedic events.

5. Hortus Botanicus: One of the world's oldest botanical gardens is the Hortus Botanicus. It has many plants and botanical gems, including rare and exotic species, and is close to the Eastern Canal Ring.

6. Weesperbuurt and Plantage Neighborhoods: Located inside the Eastern Canal Ring, the Weesperbuurt and Plantage neighborhoods provide a variety of residential areas, cultural hotspots, and open spaces. Here, you'll discover the tranquil Wertheimpark, the Jewish Historical Museum, and the Artis Royal Zoo.

7. Amstel Hotel: Since its debut in 1867, the opulent and venerable Amstel Hotel has been a benchmark for style and sophistication. It is situated on the Amstel River's banks, offers breathtaking river views, and has housed several illustrious visitors.

8. Museum Het Rembrandthuis: This Rembrandt House Museum may be close to the Eastern Canal Ring. It was formerly the home

of famed Dutch painter Rembrandt van Rijn and is now a museum featuring his studio, life, and works.

9. Stopera: The Dutch National Opera & Ballet and Amsterdam City Hall (Stadhuis) are housed in the Stopera, a well-known structure. It serves as a cultural center for opera, ballet, and governmental operations and is situated next to the Eastern Canal Ring on the Amstel River's edge.

The Eastern Canal Ring has various historical, cultural, and ecological attractions. It offers a lovely region to explore and immerse oneself in Amsterdam's rich history and cultural heritage with its beautiful canals, famous buildings, museums, and green areas.

Rembrandtplein

The lively Rembrandtplein, often known as Rembrandt Square, is situated in the center of Amsterdam. It is a well-liked tourist spot for residents and visitors named after the famed Dutch painter Rembrandt van Rijn. The following are some of Rembrandtplein's main attributes and draws:

1. Rembrandt Monument: The striking Rembrandt Monument, a bronze statue honoring the well-known artist, is in the plaza. It celebrates Rembrandt's artistic heritage and is a well-liked gathering place for tourists.

2. Rembrandtplein is renowned for its thriving nightlife and entertainment scene. Numerous pubs, clubs, cafés, and restaurants

border the area, providing a variety of places to eat, drink, and have fun.

3. Terraces & Outdoor Seating: The plaza comes alive with outdoor patios and seating spaces during the warmer months, where guests may unwind, have a beverage, and take in the bustling scene. It's a terrific place to observe people and enjoy the city's lively atmosphere.

4. Theaters: Several theaters, including the renowned Royal Theater Carré, can be found on Rembrandtplein. Theater enthusiasts may enjoy various theater acts, including plays, musicals, concerts, and comedy shows.

5. Cafes and Restaurants: The area has a variety of dining establishments, from intimate cafes to restaurants serving cuisine worldwide. Rembrandtplein has something for every taste, whether searching for a fast snack, a leisurely dinner, or a fine dining experience.

6. Shopping: Rembrandtplein and the streets surrounding it are studded with stores and boutiques that sell various goods. Visitors may browse the neighborhood for distinctive treasures, from clothing and accessories to souvenirs and Dutch delicacies.

7. Events and Festivals: Rembrandtplein holds several events and festivals annually, including live music performances, art displays, and ethnic festivities. These activities enhance the lively ambiance

and allow you to experience Amsterdam's creative and cultural landscape.

8. Convenient position: Rembrandtplein's fortunate position makes it a center for touring the rest of the city. The Flower Market, the Waterlooplein flea market, and the old canals are all accessible by foot, among other well-known sights.

Rembrandtplein in Amsterdam combines art, entertainment, food, and shopping to provide a vibrant and energetic experience. Rembrandtplein is a must-see in Amsterdam whether you're searching for a spot to unwind and take in the city's bustling ambiance, a night out on the town, or a cultural adventure.

Jordaan

Jordaan's attractive and old district is located in Amsterdam's western region. It is renowned for its winding canals, quaint neighborhoods, and bohemian vibe. Here are some of Jordaan's main characteristics and draws:

1. Canal Belt: The UNESCO-listed Canal Belt of Amsterdam includes Jordaan, which provides a beautiful view of the city's recognizable canals. The neighborhood's charming canal homes, bridges, and tree-lined canals give it a picture-postcard appearance.

2. Anne Frank House: The Anne Frank House is among the most well-known sights in Jordaan. The original structure where Anne Frank and her family hid during World War II is now home to this

museum. It offers a sobering and moving look into the Holocaust and Anne Frank's life.

3. Noordermarkt: Noordermarkt is a bustling square in Jordaan with an antique market on Mondays and a well-liked farmers market on Saturdays. Explore the stalls offering flowers, antique things, fresh fruit, organic goods, and more. The market generates a lively, energetic environment.

4. Westerkerk: The West Church, also known as the Westerkerk, is a well-known landmark in Jordaan. Its tower dominates the area and provides sweeping views of Amsterdam. Additionally, it serves as the ultimate resting place for the famed Dutch artist Rembrandt.

5. Prinsengracht: One of Amsterdam's principal waterways, the Prinsengracht Canal, passes through Jordaan. Taking in the magnificent surroundings and enjoying the lovely canal buildings while strolling along Prinsengracht is possible. Trendy shops, art galleries, and inviting cafés throughout Prinsengracht's neighborhood.

6. Houseboats: The quaint houseboats that border the canals in Jordaan are a prominent feature of the city. These floating residences enhance the neighborhood's distinctive charm. Visitors now have the opportunity to stay on several houseboats that have been transformed into lodging.

7. The Nine Streets, also known as De Negen Straatjes, are a group of charming streets that wind through Jordaan. Boutique businesses, vintage shops, art galleries, cafés, and restaurants abound on these streets. It's a shopper's paradise and a fantastic location to discover unusual and fashionable bargains.

8. Cafes, Bars, and Restaurants: Jordaan is home to many cafes, bars, and eateries that provide a wide range of delectable foods. The neighborhood has a dynamic eating scene to accommodate all tastes and preferences, ranging from traditional Dutch cuisine to foreign flavors and innovative places.

Its bohemian appeal, gorgeous canals, and creative spirit make Amsterdam's Jordaan area a favorite. It provides a variety of historical sites, thriving marketplaces, retail options, and mouthwatering food establishments. Jordaan offers a fascinating and magical experience in the center of Amsterdam, whether strolling along the canals, discovering the Nine Streets, or getting lost in the neighborhood's history.

Leidseplein

A busy square called Leidseplein may be found in the heart of Amsterdam. It offers a variety of entertainment, nightlife, eating, and retail opportunities, making it one of the city's liveliest and most exciting neighborhoods. Here are some of Leidseplein's main characteristics and draws:

1. Entertainment Locations: Leidseplein is renowned for having various entertainment locations, including theaters, movie theaters, and music venues. Famous theaters like the DeLaMar Theater and the Stadsschouwburg are located on the plaza, where you can see a broad range of acts, including plays, musicals, and comedic performances. Famous music venues like Paradiso and Melkweg showcase live performances by musicians from all over the world.

2. Vibrant nightlife: Leidseplein is well known for its exciting nightlife. It is brimming with nightlife-oriented pubs, clubs, and music venues. Numerous nightlife alternatives are available to visitors, ranging from quaint pubs and classic Dutch brown cafés to hip clubs and cocktail bars. Both residents and visitors are seeking a fun night out on the town frequent the neighborhood.

3. Street Performers: The Leidseplein is frequently crowded with street artists showing their abilities. The vibrant mood of the area is enhanced by the entertainment provided by musicians, magicians, dancers, and other performers. Visitors like to enjoy seeing these street acts.

4. Stores and Boutiques: Leidseplein and the surrounding streets provide a wide selection of boutiques and stores that appeal to various interests and preferences. There are apparel stores, gift shops, bookshops, and specialized businesses that sell one-of-a-kind goods. Additionally, the region is well-known for its diamond

shops, where you can look at and buy gorgeous jewelry and diamonds.

5. Leidseplein, a popular eating area in Amsterdam, offers various restaurants and cafés. You may choose from multiple selections, including fast snacks, traditional Dutch fare, and foreign food. The square and the streets surrounding it are dotted with cafés, eateries, and food carts, making it a fantastic spot to sate your appetite.

6. Leidsebosje is a tiny park next to Leidseplein where you may unwind and take in the scenery as you do so. It offers a serene retreat from the busy plaza and a lovely picnic or leisure walk location.

7. Proximity to Attractions and Museums: Leidseplein is ideally close to several well-known museums and attractions. Walking distance to the Rijksmuseum, Van Gogh Museum, and Stedelijk Museum makes it simple for tourists to discover Amsterdam's rich artistic and cultural legacy.

Leidseplein is a well-liked attraction for both locals and visitors due to its lively ambiance, variety of entertainment, and strategic position. Leidseplein offers a colorful and vibrant glimpse of city life in Amsterdam, whether seeking a buzzing nightlife, cultural events, shopping, or dining.

Oud-West

West of Amsterdam's city center is the vibrant and varied district known as Oud-West, which translates to "Old West" in Dutch. It is a well-liked residential area with a blend of historical allure, cultural attractions, and a lively neighborhood vibe. The following are some of Oud-West's main characteristics and draws:

1. Dining & Food: With many cafés, restaurants, and diners serving a variety of cuisines, Oud-West is renowned for its eclectic culinary scene. There are many alternatives to please your palate, from quaint neighborhood cafés to hip brunch venues. In the vicinity is also the renowned Foodhallen, a bustling indoor food market with various food vendors and a lively ambiance.

2. Vondelpark: Oud-West is next to the renowned Vondelpark, Amsterdam's biggest and most well-known park. With its beautiful green lawns, picturesque walks, ponds, and gardens, Vondelpark offers a tranquil haven in the middle of the city. A picnic, a stroll, or perhaps a bike ride are all excellent activities.

3. De Hallen: In Oud-West, a former tram depot called De Hallen has been converted into a cultural complex. It contains a variety of amenities, such as a boutique hotel, a movie theater, a library, stores, and other eating and drinking businesses. The facility frequently holds events, exhibits, and markets, enhancing the neighborhood's lively environment.

4. Ten Kate Market: Located in Oud-West, Ten Kate Market is a neighborhood street market that sells a range of fresh food, flowers, clothes, and home products. It's a beautiful location to enjoy the bustling market ambiance and buy some regional specialties.

5. Local boutiques and businesses: Several local boutiques, vintage shops, and specialized shops are sprinkled around Oud-West. Discovering unusual fashion, home goods, and design boutiques on the neighborhood's streets, such as Jan Pieter Heijestraat and Bilderdijkstraat, makes for a fun shopping experience.

6. Oud-West is home to a vibrant arts and cultural scene. You may discover modern art and local talent at the area's numerous art galleries, studios, and creative spaces. Various creative acts are also presented in theaters and other performance spaces.

7. Architectural Gems: Oud-West is known for its exquisite architecture, which includes a blend of antique structures, adorable canal cottages, and distinctive facades. Various architectural types may be seen when strolling through the neighborhood's streets, providing a window into Amsterdam's history.

8. A strong feeling of community and a local neighborhood vibe can be found in Oud-West. Various people live in the area, including families, young professionals, and artists. As you explore the site,

you'll come across neighborhood cafés, pubs, and small shops that add to the neighborhood's genuine and warm ambiance.

The district of Oud-West in Amsterdam combines culture, cuisine, shopping, and outdoor areas to create a lively and energetic atmosphere. Every traveler looking for a taste of local life will find something to do in Oud-West, whether taking a stroll around Vondelpark, discovering the neighborhood businesses, or immersing themselves in the cultural attractions.

Chapter 03
Amsterdam's Best Museums

The world-class museums in Amsterdam are famous for providing a diverse cultural and aesthetic experience. Some of Amsterdam's top museums are listed below:

Rijksmuseum

One of Amsterdam's most famous and esteemed institutions, the Rijksmuseum is regarded as one of the best art museums in the whole world. Listed below are some facts about the Rijksmuseum:

1. Art and History: The Rijksmuseum houses a sizable collection of works of art and objects from Dutch history dating back more than 800 years. The museum's collection may find masterworks by well-known Dutch artists, including Rembrandt, Vermeer, and Frans Hals. Famous works of art, including "The Night Watch" by Rembrandt and "The Milkmaid" by Vermeer, are available for viewing by visitors.

2. The Structure: The Rijksmuseum is located in a magnificent structure that is a work of art in and of itself. The museum's magnificent neo-Gothic facade and expansive interior halls, created by architect Pierre Cuypers and inaugurated in 1885, enhance the whole experience. The structure was thoroughly

repaired before reopening in 2013, blending old-world elegance with contemporary amenities.

3. Museum Organization: The museum is divided into several galleries that display various artistic movements and topics. The collection, which gives a thorough picture of Dutch art and history, consists of paintings, sculptures, decorative arts, prints, and historical artifacts.

4. The Gallery of Honor: Located in the center of the Rijksmuseum, the Gallery of Honor houses the most important and well-known pieces from the Dutch Golden Age. It is a stunning location that displays works by Rembrandt, Vermeer, and other Dutch artists, allowing visitors to comprehend the height of this time's creative achievement.

5. Asian Art: The Rijksmuseum has a fantastic collection of Asian art and Dutch artwork. Exquisite works of art from nations like China, Japan, India, and Indonesia are on show in the Asian Pavilion, which sheds light on the worldwide links and cross-cultural influences that molded Dutch history.

6. Library and Research Center: Besides a top-notch library and research center, the Rijksmuseum is also home to a wealth of information on Dutch art and history. A sizable collection of books, manuscripts, and other reference materials are kept at the library.

7. Facilities and facilities: To improve visitors' experiences, the Rijksmuseum provides several facilities, including audio guides,

guided tours, a museum store, and various food alternatives. The "Museumplein," a roomy atrium in the museum, offers a relaxing space to unwind and take at the surroundings.

8. Visiting the Rijksmuseum may fully immerse yourself in the Netherlands' rich artistic and historical legacy. The Rijksmuseum offers a fascinating voyage through Dutch art and history that can not be missed, whether you're an art fan, a history lover, or just looking for a cultural experience.

Van Gogh Museum

The world-famous Van Gogh Museum in Amsterdam is devoted to the life and works of the illustrious Dutch painter Vincent van Gogh. Here are some details on the Van Gogh Museum:

1. Vincent van Gogh's Artistic Trip: The museum takes visitors on a fascinating trip through the artist's life and evolution as an artist. Over 200 paintings, 500 sketches, and 800 letters comprise the world's most incredible collection of Van Gogh's writings, which is housed there. Van Gogh's complete body of work is represented in the group, including his earliest creations and his well-known landscapes, vivid portraits, and signature post-impressionist style.

2. Iconic works: Some of Vincent van Gogh's most well-known and significant works may be found in the Van Gogh Museum. Among the masterpieces that visitors may see are "Sunflowers," "The Bedroom," "Almond Blossom," and "Starry Night." Van Gogh's

vibrant color choices, expressive brushstrokes, and distinctive viewpoint on nature and the world around him are all clearly displayed in these works.

3. Personal Artifacts and Letters: In addition to exhibiting Van Gogh's works of art, the museum also keeps various letters and other items that provide light on his personal history and creative process. These help us better comprehend Van Gogh's problems, relationships, and artistic thinking.

4. Van Gogh's Influence: The museum examines Van Gogh's influence on later generations of painters and his effect on the art world. It also emphasizes how important his work was in influencing modern art trends.

5. Temporary Exhibits: The Van Gogh Museum frequently presents temporary exhibits that explore various facets of Van Gogh's life and work. These shows often include pieces by other artists influenced by Van Gogh or focus on specific subjects associated with his work.

6. Educational Programs and Activities: The museum provides various educational programs and activities for visitors of all ages. They include escorted tours, seminars, lectures, and family-friendly activities to engage and foster a greater understanding of Van Gogh's artwork.

7. Museum Shop and Café: The museum has a well-stocked shop where visitors may discover various items relating to Van Gogh,

including prints, books, and trinkets. Additionally, there is a café where guests may unwind and sip refreshments in a welcoming environment.

The Van Gogh Museum offers a comprehensive and illuminating look into the persona and creative genius of Vincent van Gogh. The Van Gogh Museum offers a unique and fascinating trip through the life and works of one of history's most famous artists, whether you are a fan of his career, a lover of impressionist paintings, or simply interested in learning more about the creative process of a great artist.

Anne Frank House

An important historical site and museum in Amsterdam at the Anne Frank House may be found. It is devoted to preserving the memory of young Jewish refugee Anne Frank from Nazi persecution, who penned a now-famous diary while hiding from the Nazis with her family. Here are some details on the Anne Frank House:

1. Anne Frank's Story: Visitors to the Anne Frank House may learn about Anne Frank and her family's lives and experiences during the Nazi occupation of the Netherlands. "The Diary of a Young Girl," Anne Frank's journal, gives a moving and personal account of their time in hiding. The museum emphasizes the value of tolerance, respect, and human rights while telling Anne's tale and the Holocaust's larger backdrop.

2. The museum is housed in the original structure where Anne Frank and her family hid for over two years. It was a secret room in her father's office building called the Secret Annex, hidden behind a moving bookshelf. The little residence where the Frank family lived in secrecy is one of the restored and maintained rooms that may be explored by visitors to the museum.

3. Displays and Artifacts: The Anne Frank House has several collections that provide light on Anne's life and the historical setting of her day. The museum features authentic artifacts, records, photos, and personal items belonging to Anne Frank and her family, allowing visitors to relate to their tales personally.

4. Educational Programs: For schools, teachers, and students, the Anne Frank House provides educational programs and materials. These programs use Anne Frank's tale as a springboard for discussing prejudice, racism, and human rights to foster understanding, tolerance, and empathy.

5. The Importance of Remembrance: The Anne Frank House emphasizes the significance of remembering the past and the ongoing struggle against prejudice and discrimination. To spur change and promote a more inclusive society, the museum invites visitors to consider the effects of bigotry and injustice.

6. Long Lines and Online Tickets: The Anne Frank House is a well-liked tourist destination, and because of its small size, there are

sometimes long lines. Purchasing tickets online in advance is advised to guarantee a precise admission time slot.

7. Nearby Attractions: The Anne Frank House is in the heart of Amsterdam's historic district, close to places of interest, including the Jordaan district and the Westerkerk (Western Church). Visitors may explore the neighborhood, which features shops, cafés, and attractive canal vistas.

The Anne Frank House, a potent and emotional museum, presents a rare chance to consider the effects of bigotry, the resiliency of the human spirit, and the value of preserving and learning from history. It serves as a sobering reminder of the horrors of the Holocaust and the ongoing requirement for tolerance and compassion around the globe.

Chapter 04
Practicalities

Sleeping in Amsterdam

There are a variety of lodging alternatives in Amsterdam to accommodate all tastes and price ranges. Following are some things to think about before sleeping or staying in Amsterdam:

1. Hotels: Amsterdam has many different hotels, ranging from high-end to more affordable ones. They are dispersed across the city, with numerous options available in well-liked neighborhoods, including the city center, Museumplein, and Jordaan. Making reservations in advance is a good idea, especially during busy tourist times.

2. Hostels are a popular lodging option in Amsterdam if you're on a tight budget or prefer a more communal setting. They provide private rooms and, in certain circumstances, dormitory-style rooms with shared bathrooms. In addition to often planning social events and activities, hostels are a terrific place to meet other travelers.

3. Vacation Rentals: Apartments, townhomes, and even houseboats are available for rent during your stay in Amsterdam. Various options are available for short-term visits on websites like Airbnb and Booking.com. For families or people who desire more space

and solitude, vacation rentals can offer a more homelike experience.

4. Bed and Breakfasts: Amsterdam boasts a wide selection of beautiful B&Bs, especially in residential areas like Jordaan and De Pijp. Bed and breakfasts frequently provide individualized attention, a homey setting, and an inclusive prepared meal.

5. Location: Take into account where you will be staying. Staying in the city center simplifies visiting famous sights, shopping, and enjoying the nightlife. However, living in a residential area might offer a more intimate and laid-back experience. The city's major attractions are still easily accessible even if you stay outside the city center, thanks to Amsterdam's effective public transit system.

6. Availability and Booking: Due to Amsterdam's popularity as a travel destination, it is advised to make hotel reservations well in advance, especially during busy travel times and holidays.

7. Safety and Security: Although Amsterdam is a relatively safe city, booking hotels in well-lit, central locations is always advisable. Before making a reservation, read reviews and look into the neighborhood's safety.

8. Local Tourist Taxes: Be aware that many lodging options in Amsterdam impose a local tourist tax each night; this fee is typically not included in the hotel pricing. Make sure to include this in your spending plan.

When choosing lodgings in Amsterdam, keep in mind to take into account your tastes, spending limit, and the reason for your trip. There are accommodations to meet diverse demands and guarantee a comfortable stay in the city, including hotels, hostels, vacation rentals, and bed and breakfasts.

Eating and Drinking in Amsterdam

The food scene in Amsterdam is broad and offers both traditional Dutch cuisine and various other cuisines. To help you dine and drink in Amsterdam, here are some tips:

1. Dutch cuisine: Don't miss the chance to sample some typical Dutch foods. Try treats like haring (raw herring), poffertjes (small pancakes), bitter ballen (deep-fried meatballs), and stroopwafels (caramel-filled waffles). Additionally, you may sample regional cheeses like Gouda and Edam.

2. Street Food: The culture of street food in Amsterdam is well-known. Discover the many food kiosks and stalls, especially in prominent locations like Albert Cuypmarkt, Foodhallen, and the other street markets. Try regional delicacies, including stroopwafels, poffertjes, raw herring sandwiches, and Indonesian cuisine.

3. Indonesian Cuisine: Amsterdam has a lot of Indonesian influence, so try some Indonesian cuisine. A well-liked choice is the "rice table," which serves various miniature Indonesian meals with rice.

4. Global Cuisine: As a cosmopolitan city, Amsterdam offers various international cuisines. You may choose from multiple cuisines, from South American and Mediterranean to Asian and Middle Eastern.

5. Dining by the Canals: Dine at one of the numerous canal-side cafés or restaurants to take in the quaint atmosphere of Amsterdam's canals. These places provide beautiful views as you enjoy your dinner or a drink.

6. The Brown Cafés Discover the warm and classic ambiance of the brown cafés in Amsterdam, which are typical Dutch bars. These places are renowned for their laid-back atmosphere, wooden decor, and regional brews. They are beautiful locations to relax and take in the local culture.

7. Coffee Shops: Coffee shops in Amsterdam aren't simply locations to grab a cup of coffee; they're also places where you may buy and consume cannabis products legally. Suppose you're curious about learning more about this facet of Amsterdam culture, research and pick a renowned coffee shop that welcomes residents and visitors.

8. Craft Beer and Gin: The craft beer sector in Amsterdam is thriving, with several brewers and beer pubs serving a variety of domestic and foreign craft brews. Gin is gaining popularity again; some pubs and distilleries only serve this alcohol.

9. Make reservations: Busy restaurants in Amsterdam, particularly on weekends and at prime dinner times, may get crowded.

Booking reservations in advance is a good idea, especially for popular dining establishments.

10. Water: You may save money by refilling your water bottle rather than buying bottled water, as tap water in Amsterdam is safe to drink and delicious.

Amsterdam provides a superb gastronomic experience, blending regional specialties, world cuisines, and distinctive eating venues. Savour the delicacies the city offers while exploring its unique cuisine scene.

Smoking

"Tobacco smoking" and "cannabis smoking" are used interchangeably in Amsterdam. Here are some details about both:

1. Tobacco Smoking: More stringent laws in the Netherlands have recently been implemented concerning tobacco smoking. Smoking is prohibited in most restaurants, cafés, pubs, and hotels. However, certain restaurants may have dedicated smoking rooms or outdoor terraces. In addition, smoking is typically permitted in private areas like rental flats or certain hotel rooms. Respecting the policies and procedures of your particular establishment is crucial.

2. Coffee Shops and Cannabis: Amsterdam is known for its coffee shops, where cannabis products may be bought and consumed. Cannabis is legal and controlled in the Netherlands. These businesses are allowed to sell cannabis in small amounts for

individual use. It's vital to remember that smoking marijuana is only permitted in specified locations within coffee shops and that it is legally forbidden to do so anywhere else in public, including on the sidewalks, in parks, and when using public transportation.

3. Vaping: Using electronic cigarettes or other vaping apparatus is essentially permitted in Amsterdam under the same restrictions as tobacco usage. It is essential to inquire for clarification or pay attention to any posted notices because certain businesses may have particular regulations about vaping.

4. Cannabis Edibles: Another option if you'd rather not smoke is to try cannabis edibles. These are cannabis-infused edibles, including candies, brownies, and cookies. Cannabis edibles provide a different way to consume cannabis and are available in authorized coffee shops.

In Amsterdam, it's necessary to abide by local rules and laws. Always ask about their smoking policy and be aware of the laws in various businesses and public areas. Additionally, remember that smoking rules and legislation are subject to change, so it's best to be informed of the most recent regulations while you're there.

Amsterdam with Children

Amsterdam is a family-friendly city with lots of kid-friendly activities and attractions. Here are some ideas for family-friendly activities in Amsterdam:

1. Museums: There are several kid-friendly museums in Amsterdam. Children may explore and learn about science and technology at the hands-on NEMO Science Museum. Another interactive museum that encourages kids to participate in scientific investigations and activities is the Science Center NEMO. Check out the Maritime Museum and the Tropenmuseum Junior for fun and informative activities.

2. Vondelpark: The largest and most well-known park in Amsterdam, Vondelpark is great for families. Playgrounds, picnic areas, ponds, and a paddling pool are available in the summer. Families frequently go roller skating or rent bicycles to explore the area.

3. Artis Royal Zoo: The Artis Royal Zoo, situated in the Plantage district, is an excellent location for kids to learn about diverse creatures worldwide. A planetarium, an aquarium, a butterfly pavilion, and different animal exhibits are all part of the zoo.

4. Natura Artis Magistra: This complex houses the Micropia Museum, which is devoted to germs and microorganisms, and the Artis Royal Zoo. Children may learn about the fantastic world of tiny organisms at Micropia, an interactive museum.

5. Pancake Restaurants: Several pancake restaurants in Amsterdam serve a range of mouthwatering pancakes ideal for a family lunch. Two well-liked choices are The Pancake Bakery and Pancakes Amsterdam.

6. Canal Boat Tours: Take a family-friendly canal boat trip to discover the city's well-known waterways. While sailing around the channels, these trips provide a unique view of Amsterdam's architecture and landmarks.

7. Nemo's Underwater Playground: Specifically created for kids six and younger, Nemo's Underwater Playground is housed inside the NEMO Science Museum. It is interactive displays and water-based activities offer young children a fascinating experience.

8. Riding a bike: Amsterdam is renowned for its cycling culture, and renting bikes is an excellent opportunity to take kids on a city tour. Families can conveniently travel the city on two wheels thanks to the many rental businesses that provide child seats, trailers, and unique cycles for youngsters.

9. Pannenkoekenboot: Families may enjoy unlimited pancakes while traveling through the canals of Amsterdam on the Pannenkoekenboot (Pancake Boat), a unique eating experience. It combines sightseeing with eating delicious pancakes.

10. Playgrounds and Play Places: Amsterdam has several gardens and plays places. Examples of parks with kid-friendly playgrounds are Oosterpark, Westerpark, and Beatrixpark.

Remember to tailor your activities to the interests and ages of your kids. Families with kids will appreciate visiting Amsterdam since it offers a range of alternatives that may accommodate diverse tastes.

Bicycling in Amsterdam

A well-liked and famous method to see Amsterdam is by bicycle. The following are some essential details concerning riding in Amsterdam:

1. Amsterdam is renowned for having a robust and well-developed bike infrastructure. There are designated bike lanes in the city that are set off from automobile traffic by curbs or painted markers. Staying in the designated bike lanes and abiding by bicycle road regulations is essential.

2. Renting a bike: In Amsterdam, there are many rental shops spread out over the city, making it simple to hire a bike. Your choices include Standard, electric, cargo, and even tandem bicycles. Before renting, comparing costs and inspecting the bikes' condition is wise because rental fees might vary.

3. Bike Sharing: Amsterdam also features bike-sharing programs, including OV-fiets (a service for sharing bicycles for public transit) and several commercial bike-sharing businesses. These programs let you borrow a bike for a limited time and return it to a predetermined spot. Check the individual bike-sharing service's availability, registration requirements, and price information.

4. Riding Etiquette: Because of the distinctive riding culture in Amsterdam, it's essential to understand the basic rules of the road. Use hand signals to communicate your intentions, stay on the right side of the bike lane, and pay attention to other cyclists,

pedestrians, and moving cars. When leaving your bike alone, make sure it is properly locked.

5. Safety: Cycling is typically safe in Amsterdam, but you should still use caution. For your protection, put on a helmet, mainly if you're not used to cycling in congested urban areas, and watch out for tram tracks because bike wheels might get caught in them. Look for other bikers, people on foot, and vehicles, especially at junctions and crowded places.

6. Bike theft: Unfortunately, bike theft is a widespread problem in Amsterdam. To attach your bike to a stationary item, such as a bike rack, use a strong lock (ideally a double lock). Avoid leaving expensive stuff on your bike; if insurance is offered, consider getting it. Taking a picture or writing down the bike's serial number is also a smart idea for future use.

7. Bike Parking: There are several places to store your bike in Amsterdam, including designated racks, parking garages, and even floating bike stations. Pour your bike in these spots to prevent obstructing walkways or pedestrian zones.

8. Traffic Regulations: Become familiar with the area's bicycle-specific traffic regulations and signage. Pay attention to traffic signs, give way to pedestrians, and ride your bike in the general direction of traffic.

A handy and enjoyable way to tour Amsterdam's streets, canals, and districts is by bicycle. You may have a fantastic bike experience in this bicycle-friendly city with the proper knowledge of cycling etiquette, safety precautions, and infrastructure.

What to Buy in Amsterdam

Numerous distinctive, regionally produced goods are available in Amsterdam, making excellent presents or souvenirs. Here are a few well-liked products to think about purchasing in Amsterdam:

1. Dutch Cheese: Delicious cheeses are a specialty of Amsterdam. Edam and Gouda are particularly well-liked options. The city is filled with cheese businesses that provide a broad range of tastes and ages. Transporting items back home is made simple by vacuum-sealed packaging.

2. Netherlands Clogs: The "klompen," or traditional wooden clogs, are a well-known representation of Dutch culture. They come in various shapes and styles, from conventional to contemporary. They are available at souvenir shops and specialty clog shops.

3. Dutch Gin (Jenever): Gin precedes Jenever, a classic Dutch alcoholic beverage. It is available in various tastes and types and is frequently consumed plain or in cocktails. Look for specialist liquor stores or distilleries to find a bottle of this traditional Dutch beverage.

4. Delftware. Although it originated in the city of Delft, Delftware, also known as Delft Blue, is a form of blue and white pottery strongly linked to Dutch culture. Look for hand-painted ceramic items with exquisite designs, such as plates, vases, and tiles.

5. The Netherlands is renowned for its delectable chocolates. Look for chocolate stores that provide many flavors and designs, such as truffles, pralines, and classic Dutch chocolate bars. Tony's Chocolonely and Van Velze's Chocolaterie are well-known chocolate manufacturers in Amsterdam.

6. Dutch Liquorice: The Netherlands has a long heritage of producing licorice sweets, including sweet, salty, and even salty-sweet varieties, so if you're a fan, you'll find a broad array of alternatives in Amsterdam. Discover your neighborhood candy stores to try this particular Dutch confection.

7. Stroopwafels: Stroopwafels are chewy, thin waffles with a syrup filling that resembles caramel. They make a delectable snack or souvenir and are a particular Dutch delight. Visit your neighborhood markets or specialized stores to find freshly produced or pre-packaged stroopwafels.

8. Vintage & Antiques: You may find one-of-a-kind vintage goods and antiques in Amsterdam's many flea markets and antique stores. These markets and shops provide a treasure trove, whether you're seeking antique apparel, old-fashioned books, retro furniture, or one-of-a-kind souvenirs.

9. Bicycle Accessories: Amsterdam, a city known for its cycling culture, provides bicycles with a choice of clothing and accessories. To bring home a valuable and fashionable gift, look for elegant bike bells, bike lights, bike bags, or even cycling-themed clothes.

10. Art and Prints: Amsterdam is well-known for its art scene, and you can find several art galleries and stores that sell a variety of paintings and prints. You may discover artwork that perfectly captures the creative energy of Amsterdam, from modern pieces to classic Dutch landscapes.

To locate unique and genuine things, don't forget to browse local markets, independent shops, and specialized stores. You may take some Dutch culture home by purchasing souvenirs in Amsterdam, whether foods, drinks, crafts, or cultural objects. This will help you to remember your trip to Amsterdam forever.

Entertainment in Amsterdam

Amsterdam has a thriving and varied entertainment scene that can accommodate a range of hobbies and tastes. You may enjoy the following well-liked sorts of entertainment in the city:

1. Live Music: The live music scene in Amsterdam is growing, with venues featuring a variety of musical genres and styles. You may catch performances by local musicians and well-known international performers everywhere, from tiny, cozy jazz bars to bigger concert venues. Bimhuis, Melkweg, and Paradiso are popular places to hear live music.

2. Theater & Performing Arts: Amsterdam is home to a vibrant theatrical scene, with several theaters displaying a variety of productions, including plays, musicals, dance performances, and comedy acts. Among the notable venues in the city are the Royal

Theater Carré, DeLaMar Theater, and the Dutch National Opera & Ballet.

3. Nightlife and Clubs: Amsterdam offers various pubs and venues to suit multiple preferences. The city has everything from comfortable pubs to hip cocktail bars and exciting nightclubs. Popular nightlife hotspots include the Rembrandtplein and Leidseplein neighborhoods.

4. Film & Cinema: Amsterdam offers a wide selection of theaters and film festivals for movie buffs. The renowned Pathé Tuschinski theater features a rich movie-going environment built in the Art Deco style. Several film festivals are also held in the city, including the Amsterdam Film Festival and the International Documentary Film Festival Amsterdam (IDFA).

5. Comedy Clubs: Amsterdam has several comedy clubs that regularly feature stand-up performances in both English and Dutch. You may catch live comedic acts at well-known locations, including The Comedy Café and Boom Chicago.

6. Gambling and casinos: There are several casinos in Amsterdam where you may test your luck at several games, including slot machines, roulette, blackjack, and poker. The city's primary casino, Holland Casino Amsterdam, has a variety of gambling possibilities.

7. Festivals & Events: Amsterdam holds a variety of festivals and events all year long that appeal to various interests. These range from music festivals to culinary festivals to cultural festivals.

Among the most well-known yearly events in the city are the King's Day celebration on April 27 and the Amsterdam Dance Event (ADE).

8. Escape Rooms: There are several escape rooms in Amsterdam where you and your friends may work together to solve puzzles and riddles to leave a themed room within a set amount of time. Your ability to solve problems will be put to the test by this enjoyable and engaging activity.

9. Sports and recreation: Amsterdam has many sports and leisure activities. You may rent a boat to tour the city's canals, sign up for a cycling tour with a guide, go for a jog or bike ride in a park, or even try indoor activities like trampoline parks or indoor climbing.

These are just a few illustrations of Amsterdam's entertainment alternatives. Whether you're interested in music, theater, nightlife, or cultural activities, the city has something to offer everyone. To find entertainment that meets your interests, check out the neighborhood listings for events, talk to the residents for suggestions, and ask about them.

Free or Almost Free

There are many opportunities to enjoy Amsterdam without breaking the bank if you seek free or inexpensive activities. Here are a few ideas:

1. Explore the Canals: Amsterdam's canal belt's UNESCO World Heritage site offers stunning views. Walk gently along the canals,

over the gorgeous bridges, and admire the city's distinctive architecture.

2. Visit Free Museums: A few museums in Amsterdam provide free access on certain days or during certain hours. Visitors under 18 are admitted free to the Stedelijk Museum, while holders of the I Amsterdam City Card are admitted free to the Amsterdam Museum. Additionally free to view is the shuttersgalerij, housed at the Amsterdam Museum.

3. Use the Parks: Amsterdam has several lovely parks where you can unwind, picnic, or stroll. Popular options include Vondelpark, Westerpark, and Oosterpark. These parks frequently host free activities, in-person shows, and outdoor exhibits during the summer.

4. Free Walking Tours: A free walking tour is a fantastic way to discover a city's history and culture. Many businesses provide guided tours that let you see various areas and sites; tips pay the guides.

5. Enjoy the Street Art: The street art culture in Amsterdam is thriving. Explore areas like NDSM-Werf in Amsterdam-Noord or the Jordaan district to find vibrant murals and graffiti. A self-guided walking tour is another option for discovering the street art scattered across the city.

6. Visit Free Markets: The Albert Cuyp Market, the city's biggest outdoor market, is a terrific spot to soak up the ambiance and

peruse various merchandise and food booths. In addition, a variety of vintage goods, apparel, and antiques are available at the Waterlooplein Flea Market.

7. Attend Free Events: Keep an eye out for free events, such as concerts, festivals, and cultural gatherings, that are taking place in Amsterdam. The Open Air Theatre in the Vondelpark is one of the parks and squares where you can see outdoor music and shows throughout the summer.

8. Ride a bike or stroll around Amsterdamse Bos, a sizable park outside the city. It provides lovely parks, jogging routes, and bike lanes. The natural splendor of this urban forest may be discovered by renting a bike or going for a lengthy walk.

9. Go to the Begijnhof: This secret courtyard in the middle of the city provides a tranquil haven from the busy streets. It's old buildings and peaceful ambiance make it free to explore and give visitors a look into Amsterdam's past.

10. Take a Ferry: Take a free ferry from Amsterdam Central Station to Amsterdam-Noord's adjacent neighborhoods. The boats allow you to explore the lively and artistic area across the IJ River and provide beautiful city views.

For any activity or place you intend to visit, don't forget to double-check the opening times and any applicable limits or rules. You can maximize your time in Amsterdam without breaking the bank with little planning and study.

Amsterdam Connections

Amsterdam, a significant transportation hub, provides several links to other cities inside and outside the Netherlands. You may reach the following primary connections from Amsterdam:

1. Schiphol Airport: Schiphol Airport in Amsterdam is one of the busiest airports in Europe and a significant global hub. From here, you may take a direct or a connecting flight to many locations worldwide.

2. Train Connections: The city's primary train station, Amsterdam Centraal, offers good rail service to several locations around the Netherlands and its neighbors. Cities like Brussels, Paris, London, and Cologne are connected to Amsterdam by fast trains like the Thalys and Eurostar. The Nederlandse Spoorwegen (NS)-run Dutch railway system also provides frequent domestic connections to Rotterdam, The Hague, Utrecht, and Eindhoven.

3. Public transit: Amsterdam has a robust public transit system connecting various city sections and surrounding areas. This system includes trams, buses, and metros. These services, run by the GVB (Municipal Transport Company), make getting around Amsterdam and taking in the adjacent cities and attractions simple.

4. Canal Boat Tours: Amsterdam's famous canals offer a distinctive transportation and city exploration mode. You may view the sights and monuments of Amsterdam from a new angle by taking one of the many canal excursions offered by boat tour companies. These

excursions frequently comment on and explain the city's past and present.

5. Bike Rentals: Renting a bike is a simple way to move around and experience Amsterdam, recognized as a bicycle-friendly city. You may hire a bike from one of the numerous rental businesses in the area and travel about Amsterdam and its environs using the massive network of bike lanes and pathways.

6. Car Rentals: Renting a car allows you to venture outside of Amsterdam if you prefer to see the Netherlands at your speed. The Dutch road network is well-maintained and links Amsterdam to other cities and areas. There are several vehicle rental agencies situated in and around the city.

7. River Cruises: For river cruises on the Rhine, Main, and Danube rivers, Amsterdam is a typical starting or finishing point. With the convenience of a floating hotel, these cruises allow travelers to tour various European nations and towns, including Germany, Austria, Hungary, and more.

Amsterdam's strong connections make it simple to reach many locations and continue your adventure inside the Netherlands and abroad, whether you want to travel by plane, rail, boat, bike, or vehicle.

Chapter 05:
SIDE TRIPS FROM AMSTERDAM

Side excursions from Amsterdam provide an excellent chance to discover the Netherlands outside its energetic city. These outings offer the ideal respite from the bustle of the city, whether you're a fan of nature, history, or art.

Just a short distance from Amsterdam, the lovely city of Haarlem enchants travelers with its enduring beauty and extensive past. Haarlem, one of the oldest cities in the Netherlands, is a great place to spend a day trip because of its abundance of architectural marvels, cultural riches, and relaxed environment.

Entering Haarlem is like stepping into a picture book. The city's charming atmosphere results from the well-preserved medieval buildings, cobblestone streets, and peaceful canals. You may see spectacular specimens of Gothic and Renaissance architecture while strolling around the city's historic core, such as the well-known Grote Kerk (Great Church), which has a tall spire and an opulent interior.

They were long recognized as a center for the arts and culture of Haarlem. Frans Hals and Jacob van Ruisdael were two well-known painters from the Dutch Golden Age who were born and raised in the city. By visiting the Frans Hals Museum, which has an extraordinary collection of Dutch Golden Age paintings, including works by Hals himself, art fans may fully immerse themselves in Haarlem's creative past.

Aside from its rich artistic history, Haarlem is known for its bustling market squares like the Grote Markt, where locals and tourists congregate to enjoy outdoor cafés, try regional cuisine, and enjoy the energetic atmosphere. The impressive Stadhuis (City Hall), a spectacular Renaissance structure contributing to the city's appeal, dominates the square.

Beyond its marvels of architecture and culture, Haarlem is surrounded by stunning scenery. The city is located in an area noted for its tulip fields, providing a vibrant scene in the spring. A local attraction called Keukenhof Gardens offers a delightful chance to immerse yourself in a sea of blooming flowers. Millions of tulips, daffodils, and hyacinths combine to form a stunning panorama.

With its many attractions and inviting environment, Haarlem is a beautiful place to visit as a side trip from Amsterdam. Inviting you to experience its distinctive fusion of history, culture, and natural beauty, Haarlem offers a lovely retreat from the bustle and noise of the city, whether you're wandering along its canals, touring its museums, or just indulging in the local food and bustling cafe scene.

Delft

The picturesque city of Delft, situated in the southwest of the Netherlands, is well-known for its long history, signature blue-and-white ceramics, and ties to Dutch painter Johannes Vermeer. Delft offers tourists a fascinating excursion into the nation's cultural past with its charming canals, well-conserved buildings, and laid-back atmosphere.

Its historical significance becomes apparent as you stroll through the city's gorgeous squares and cobblestone streets. A picture-perfect scene is created in Delft's Old Town by the gabled buildings, tiny passageways, and tree-lined canals. The city's focal point is the magnificent Nieuwe Kerk (New Church), a Gothic masterpiece that holds the tombs of the Dutch royal family members and provides panoramic views from its tower.

The famous Delftware pottery, made in the city for generations, is well-known worldwide. Ceramics in the characteristic blue-and-white style are prized for their fine craftsmanship and elaborate motifs. The Royal Delft factory, the last surviving Delftware factory from the 17th century, offers visitors a look into the world of Delftware. You may observe the conventional production methods here and tour the museum to discover the background and significance of this cherished art form.

Delft has an additional charm due to its connection to the famous painter Johannes Vermeer. One of the finest painters of the Dutch Golden Age, Vermeer, was born and raised in Delft. The Vermeer Centrum Delft, a museum devoted to his works, allows visitors to study Vermeer's life and career while learning about his methods and his influence on the art world.

The bustling Markt square in Delft is the center of the action and is home to the impressive City Hall in Renaissance architecture, several eateries, and a busy market. Here, you may savor regional specialties, peruse kiosks offering crafts and fresh fruit, and enjoy the colorful ambiance. Take a leisurely canal boat trip to experience the city's splendor differently.

Due to its small size and walker-friendly design, Delft is the ideal city to explore on foot or by bicycle. Delft has tranquil parks, green areas, and quaint districts outside the historic district just waiting to be explored.

Delft allows tourists to travel back in time and immerse themselves in the rich cultural fabric of the Netherlands with its intriguing combination of history, art, and traditional craftsmanship. Delft provides a remarkable and captivating experience highlighting the nation's distinctive past, whether you're admiring its architectural marvels, discovering the world of Delftware, or getting in touch with Vermeer's creative legacy.

The Bulb Fields

Visitors come worldwide to see the spectacular natural phenomenon known as the Bulb Fields in the Netherlands. The bulb fields are famed for their beautiful and expansive displays of tulips, daffodils, hyacinths, and other colorful spring flowers. They are primarily seen in the area known as the "Bollenstreek," which spans from Haarlem to Leiden.

The fields explode with color from late March to mid-May, converting the surroundings into a fascinating tapestry of blooms. It is incredible to witness unending rows of flowering flowers extending as far as the eye perceives. The fields are beautifully tended, displaying several bulb kinds in thoughtfully planned arrangements to create a fantastic color mosaic.

The bulb fields provide a singular opportunity to appreciate nature's splendor and the Netherlands' rich floral history. Walking or riding a bicycle along the approved trails that meander across the countryside allows visitors to explore the fields. The air is filled with the aroma of the blooms, making for a sensory encounter that is both aesthetically gorgeous and enticingly fragrant.

The "Garden of Europe," Keukenhof, is one of the most well-known locations for bulb fields. Keukenhof is a huge park close to Lisse with millions of blooms, breathtaking displays, and well-planned gardens.

Visitors may stroll through themed gardens, marvel at elaborate floral arrangements, and take fantastic pictures amidst the sea of petals.

The bulb fields not only offer a visual feast, but they also shed light on the long-standing flower-growing history in the Netherlands. The nation is well known worldwide for its skill in growing bulbs and exporting flowers. Visitors may learn about the development of bulb cultivation and its methods by visiting nearby farms, museums, and educational facilities.

The bulb fields are more than a springtime draw; they also represent rebirth and the approach of the warmer months. They are now recognized as a symbol of Dutch culture and a well-liked travel destination, drawing tourists worldwide.

Exploring the bulb fields's a magical experience since it enables people to realize how beautiful nature is whole. The bulb fields provide a memorable and aesthetically spectacular excursion into the center of the Netherlands' floral legacy, whether you are an enthusiastic flower enthusiast, a photography lover, or simply seeking a tranquil respite amidst bright surroundings.

Rotterdam

The second-largest city in the Netherlands, Rotterdam, is a lively, modern metropolis with striking architecture, a thriving arts scene, and a forward-thinking attitude. Rotterdam provides tourists with a distinctive and enthralling experience. It is renowned for its innovative urban architecture and rich nautical heritage.

The city's magnificent skyline, which features a variety of architectural marvels, is one of its distinguishing features. With renowned structures like the Cube Houses, the Euromast Tower, and the Markthal, a unique horseshoe-shaped market hall covered in colorful murals, the Rotterdam skyline combines modern and experimental ideas. Architecture fans will appreciate the city's dedication to pushing limits and cutting-edge designs.

The maritime legacy of Rotterdam is a significant part of its identity. The city's ancient port, once the busiest in Europe, was essential to global trade. The Rotterdam Port District, an urban waterfront region, has grown out of the seaport in modern times. Visitors may join a boat excursion, explore this vibrant neighborhood, or visit the Nautical Museum to see the busy nautical activities firsthand.

For those who enjoy art and culture, the city is a paradise. An excellent collection of paintings by famous Dutch artists like Rembrandt and Van Gogh may be seen in the Museum Boijmans Van Beuningen. Various contemporary art shows are available at the Kunsthal Rotterdam, and the Witte de Withstraat is a bustling street studded with galleries, shops, and hip cafes.

The city of Rotterdam exhibits a dedication to innovation and sustainability. The breathtaking architectural wonder known as Rotterdam Central Station is a transportation hub with sustainable design characteristics. The city is a leader in sustainable urban development since it is also home to many sustainable initiatives, such as urban rooftop farms, eco-friendly buildings, and a vast network of bike lanes.

Rotterdam will be a gastronomic pleasure for foodies. Because of the city's diverse population, many international cuisines are available. Rotterdam is a food lover's heaven, with Michelin-starred restaurants and hip food markets.

The lively nightlife of Rotterdam adds to its attractiveness. The city has several pubs, clubs, and music venues that may accommodate different preferences, making for an exciting and lively night out.

Rotterdam has much to offer everyone, whether you're interested in modern architecture, maritime history, or searching out cultural and gastronomic excursions. Visitors seeking to experience the leading edge of Dutch culture and urban architecture will find it attractive thanks to its inventive spirit, vibrant environment, and distinctive combination of heritage and innovation.

Utrecht

The delightful city of Utrecht, situated in the center of the Netherlands, is well-known for its extensive history, beautiful canals, and thriving cultural scene. Utrecht, one of the oldest towns in the nation, provides tourists with the ideal fusion of ancient sites, priceless works of art, and a buzzing environment.

The renowned Dom Tower, the highest church tower in the Netherlands, serves as the city's focal point. The building's stunning 360-degree views of Utrecht's picturesque canals, roofs, and surroundings are available by climbing. Visitors are welcome to discover the historical beauty of Utrecht's medieval city center, distinguished by its winding lanes, magnificent canal wharves, and well-maintained buildings.

Another reason Utrecht is well-known is for its extensive canal system, which is comparable to Amsterdam's. You may enjoy the city's distinctive architecture and get a new perspective on Utrecht's charm by boat excursion through the canals. Indulge in the bustling atmosphere of the waterfront cafés, restaurants, and stores while strolling along the beautiful Oudegracht (Old Canal).

Art and culture are in vogue in Utrecht, home to several top-notch museums and cultural organizations. The Centraal Museum exhibits various artwork, including pieces by Dutch artists like Dick Bruna, the man behind Miffy, and Gerrit Rietveld. The Railway Museum takes visitors on a fascinating tour through the history of railroads, while the Museum Speelklok is a singular museum devoted to self-playing musical instruments.

Another attraction is Utrecht's thriving music culture, which features live performances at numerous locations around the city. Various concerts and events are held in the TivoliVredenburg, a contemporary music hall complex that draws domestic and foreign performers.

Since Utrecht Academic, one of the oldest and biggest institutions in the Netherlands, is located there, the city is well known for its vibrant academic culture. The city's fashionable cafés, bookshops, and boutiques reflect its youthful vitality, fostering a lively and international atmosphere.

The parks and natural spaces of Utrecht will appeal to nature enthusiasts. You may find tranquil getaways in the Griftpark, Wilhelminapark, and Julianapark, where you can unwind, picnic, or engage in outdoor activities. Utrecht is a great place to start a bike and hiking adventure because it is surrounded by stunning scenery.

Utrecht provides tourists with an enthralling experience with its combination of history, culture, and vibrant atmosphere. Utrecht's friendly and inviting attitude guarantees a memorable and pleasurable visit, whether touring its historical sites, immersing yourself in art and music, or just taking in the laid-back Dutch lifestyle.

Chapter 06
3-DAY TRIPS
DAY 1: North of Amsterdam

For those looking for a new viewpoint on the Netherlands, the north of Amsterdam has many sites and experiences worth investigating. This area offers a lot, from attractive towns and breathtaking scenery to historic landmarks and cultural treasures.

Alkmaar & Zaanse Schans

Two lovely towns north of Amsterdam, Alkmaar and Zaanse Schans, provide tourists with a view of the Netherlands' rich cultural history and gorgeous scenery.

The historic cheese market in Alkmaar, sometimes called the "Cheese City," has existed since the sixteenth century. The market, which takes place on Fridays from April to September, honors the long-standing custom of weighing, exchanging, and moving cheese. The big wheels of cheese are carried and considered by cheese bearers, who are costumed in traditional garb, providing spectators with a colorful spectacle. The market square, surrounded by historical structures, is a busy gathering place where tourists can buy a variety of Dutch cheeses, try regional specialties, and take in the energetic atmosphere.

Alkmaar has a beautiful old town with attractive canals, winding lanes, and well-preserved houses in addition to the cheese market. Visit the Stedelijk Museum Alkmaar, which displays a collection of Dutch Golden Age paintings and objects that showcase the city's rich past, and take a stroll around the streets and secret courtyards of the town.

Zaanse Schans, a living outdoor museum that provides a fascinating look into Dutch history and traditional crafts, is located near Alkmaar. This distinctive community features painstakingly preserved wooden homes, windmills, and artist studios that honor the area's industrial past. Visitors may see windmill interiors, observe traditional crafts like cheese- and clog-making in action, and visit historical museums to learn more about the region's industrial heritage. Zaanse Schans is a stunning location for photography enthusiasts and history fans alike due to its lovely surroundings and distinctive windmills bordering the banks of the Zaan River.

Alkmaar and Zaanse Schans both provide a pleasant diversion from the hectic metropolis of Amsterdam. These locations offer a unique chance to become immersed in Dutch customs, craftsmanship, and the nation's rich cultural history because of its historical allure, cultural attractions, and scenic beauty.

Edam, Volendam & Marken

Three charming towns to the north of Amsterdam—Edam, Volendam, and Marken—offer travelers a window into the old-world way of life, breathtaking scenery, and cultural history of the Dutch.

Edam is a lovely town distinguished by its well-preserved 17th-century architecture and attractive canals. It is famous across the world for its peculiar cheese. Visit the famed Cheese Market, where you can see the centuries-old custom of weighing and trading cheese, and stroll around the town's cobblestone streets, admiring the charming homes. Please don't miss the opportunity to sample the delectable Edam cheese and see the local cheese stores and museums to discover more about its manufacturing.

The bustling fishing community of Volendam, which is situated on the IJsselmeer, is well known for its quaint atmosphere and active harbor. The village is a well-liked tourist attraction because of its vibrant buildings, wooden boats, and busy waterfront. Visit the Volendams Museum to learn about the history and culture of the area, wander the picturesque alleyways, and indulge in mouthwatering fresh seafood dishes at one of the numerous eateries around the port. Don't forget to grab the ideal shot while wearing one of the many stores in the area that hire authentic Dutch attire.

A little island community called Marken provides a window into the area's customary way of life of farming and fishing. Marken, an island connected to the mainland by a causeway, is well-known for its attractive wooden cottages, winding alleyways, and recognizable lighthouse at the village's entrance. Visit the Marker Museum to learn about the island's history and nautical customs, wander leisurely around the hamlet, and enjoy the tranquil ambiance and stunning ocean views.

Cycling through the picturesque pathways that connect Edam, Volendam, and Marken is another well-liked method of discovering these places. The stunning scenery, which includes windmills, dykes, and vast meadows, serves as the perfect background for your adventure.

These three locations provide a unique chance to explore the attractive architecture, learn about the traditional Dutch way of life, and enjoy regional specialties. Edam, Volendam, and Marken are beautiful locations to visit and discover, whether captivated by cheese, curious about fishing towns, or simply wanting a look into the Dutch cultural history.

Hoorn, Enkhuizen & the Historic Triangle

The Historic Triangle, Hoorn, and Enkhuizen make up a fascinating area in the north of Amsterdam that transports tourists back in time while highlighting the nautical heritage, extensive history, and scenic landscapes of the Netherlands.

The ancient city of Hoorn, situated on the IJsselmeer, was important during the Dutch Golden Age. Its attractive old town, well-preserved port, and buildings from the 17th century serve as reminders of its illustrious maritime past. Visit the Westfries Museum to learn about the city's history, stroll through the cobblestoned streets, and climb the Hoofdtoren, a defense tower from the Middle Ages, for sweeping views.

Another jewel in the area, Enkhuizen, was a famous harbor during the Dutch Golden Age. The city is renowned for its historic district, where you may meander through winding alleyways dotted with exquisitely restored structures. Visit the Zuiderzee Museum to see traditional crafts, old structures, and marine relics while learning about life in and around the former Zuiderzee (now IJsselmeer). With its spectacular ancient ships and lively atmosphere, Enkhuizen's harbor provides a window into the area's nautical past.

The link between Hoorn, Enkhuizen, and the neighboring town of Medemblik is called the Historic Triangle. The Dutch East India

Company (VOC) historically had strongholds in these three towns, constituting a crucial commercial route known as the "Triangle Trade." Taking the old steam railway from Hoorn to Medemblik, then taking the leisurely boat from Medemblik to Enkhuizen, will take visitors on an unforgettable voyage. This picturesque route lets you experience the environment, observe how it changes, and learn about the area's maritime history.

You'll pass through picturesque scenery, marvel at windmills, cruise through the IJsselmeer's vast seas, and take in the splendor of the Dutch countryside along the route. The area's history, architecture, and culture are explored differently at each station along the Historic Triangle.

Hoorn, Enkhuizen, and the Historic Triangle provide a rich and immersive experience, whether you're fascinated by nautical history, drawn to well-preserved historic cities, or just looking for a calm drive through the Dutch countryside. This area offers a fascinating window into the history of the Netherlands and its ongoing relationship with the sea, whether you want to stroll through centuries-old neighborhoods or sail on ancient waterways.

Flevoland

The Dutch province of Flevoland is unusual and fascinating, known for its creative land reclamation initiatives and distinctively modern architecture. The newest area in the Netherlands is Flevoland, located in the middle of the nation. It was made possible by draining and reclaiming the old inland sea known as the IJsselmeer.

The region is renowned for its enormous open spaces, which include broad fields, navigable canals, and wildlife preserves. A sizable natural reserve in Flevoland called the Oostvaardersplassen is a sanctuary for animals and provides hiking, biking, and birding opportunities. The region is a haven for nature lovers since it is home to numerous bird species, especially migrating birds.

Flevoland is a center for cutting-edge urban design and architecture. The central city in the province, Almere, is a showcase for cutting-edge architectural ideas and modern architecture. With its eye-catching structures and innovative urban design, the town center exemplifies the goal of developing a contemporary and sustainable city. Visitors may take in the eye-catching architecture, stop by architectural hotspots like the Kunstlinie Almere Flevoland (KAF), and revel in the city's artistic flare.

The Batavia Stad Fashion Outlet in Lelystad is another notable Flevoland location. This retail center attracts residents and tourists since it offers a large selection of designer goods at affordable costs.

The Batavia and Museum in Lelystad offer information on the engineering wonders and the history of the area's land reclamation operations for anyone interested in the history of land reclamation and water management. Visitors may examine antique ships, discover the region's cultural heritage, and learn how polders are made.

Flevoland provides tourists a singular experience by fusing modernism with unspoiled nature and exhibiting Dutch urban design and land reclamation prowess. Flevoland offers an exciting and distinctive side of the Netherlands, whether you're interested in discovering avant-garde buildings, getting in touch with nature, or learning about the area's technical accomplishments.

DAY 2: South of Amsterdam

There are several desirable locations south of Amsterdam that have a blend of scenic natural areas, historic landmarks, and cultural attractions. Here are a few notable locations to check out:

Keukenhof & Aalsmeer

Two well-known locations south of Amsterdam that highlight the robust flower industry and breathtaking scenery of the Netherlands are Keukenhof and Aalsmeer.

1. Keukenhof: Situated near Lisse, Keukenhof is one of the most famous flower gardens in the world and a must-see for flower lovers. Keukenhof, which covers an area of about 79 acres, is known for its vibrant tulips, daffodils, hyacinths, and other springtime blossoms. The park offers carefully planned gardens, imaginative exhibits, and attractive floral displays. Wanderers may discover the Netherlands' horticultural heritage while taking in the aroma and beauty of millions of flowers and the country's

lovely walkways. Every year, Keukenhof is only accessible for a short period, often from mid-March to mid-May, when spring flowers bloom.

2. Aalsmeer: Also known as Bloemenveiling Aalsmeer, the Aalsmeer Flower sale is renowned. Millions of flowers and plants are exchanged daily, making it one of the world's most significant floral auction marketplaces. Visitors are welcome to join a guided tour of the auction halls to observe the hectic activity, discover the mechanics of the flower trade, and be amazed by the enormous variety of flowers from across the globe. The Aalsmeer Flower Auction offers a fascinating look into the international flower trade and its importance to the Netherlands.

Regarding the history of flowers in the Netherlands, Keukenhof, and Aalsmeer both provide distinctive experiences. These locations immerse tourists in the beauty and cultural significance of the nation's floral traditions, from the spectacular flower displays at Keukenhof to the busy flower commerce in Aalsmeer.

Leiden

An ancient and dynamic city with a rich cultural legacy and a renowned university, Leiden is south of Amsterdam. Leiden, known as the hometown of famed Dutch artist Rembrandt van Rijn, provides various attractions, including museums, canals, charming streets, and lovely parks.

1. Museums and Cultural Attractions: Leiden is home to a diverse array of museums representing an excellent collection. While the Museum Volkenkunde (Museum of Ethnology) displays artwork and artifacts from many cultures worldwide, the Rijksmuseum van Oudheden (National Museum of Antiquities) includes treasures from ancient Egypt, Greece, and Rome. Visitors interested in art can visit the Museum De Lakenhal, which features artwork by Rembrandt and other well-known Dutch artists from the 16th to the 21st century. The SieboldHuis also emphasizes Japanese art and culture. Historic structures in the city, such as the Pieterskerk (St. Peter's Church) and the Leiden Observatory, also shed light on its lengthy past.

2. Canals and the Old City: Leiden has attractive canals dotted with elegant older homes and endearing bridges. A lovely way to discover the city is to stroll along the canals. The ancient city center has boutique stores, quaint cafes, and winding lanes. Visitors love to visit the Burcht van Leiden, a medieval stronghold perched atop a hill that offers sweeping views of the city.

3. Leiden University: One of the oldest institutions in the Netherlands, Leiden University was founded in 1575 and enjoys a high academic reputation. The university's ancient structures, such as the Academy Building, enhance the city's appeal. The university's botanical garden, Hortus Botanicus, is very worthwhile and has an extensive collection of plant species.

4. Parks and Outdoor spots: Leiden has several green areas where guests can unwind and enjoy the scenery. Near the city center lies the tranquil Van der Werfpark, which features lovely gardens and a monument. The old windmill-turned-museum Molen de Valk is next to the park. Forests, lakes, and hiking routes can be found in the enormous park, The Leidense Hout, located outside the city.

Leiden attracts tourists because of its unique blend of historical significance, cultural attractions, and scenic beauty. Leiden provides a beautiful and immersive experience whether you're interested in history, art, or just wandering along lovely canals.

The Hague

The Hague, sometimes spelled Den Haag, is the seat of the Dutch government and a significant historical and cultural center. The Hague, a city on the country's western coast, is well known for its international organizations, gorgeous architecture, and active cultural scene.

1. The International Court of Justice, the International Criminal Court, and the Peace Palace are just a few of the numerous international organizations and institutions headquartered in The Hague. Visitors may tour the Peace Palace, a well-known representation of justice and peace, and discover how it helps settle conflicts worldwide. These organizations provide the city with a sense of diplomacy and international significance.

2. Binnenhof and Historical Sites: The Binnenhof, a medieval structure in the middle of The Hague, is the Netherlands' political hub. The Dutch parliament and other government structures are located there. Within the Binnenhof, the Ridderzaal (Hall of Knights), a Gothic-style structure used for state events, is an important historical location. In addition, the city is home to many historical sites, such as the Mauritshuis Museum, which is home to a famous collection of artwork from the Dutch Golden Age, including Vermeer's "Girl with a Pearl Earring."

3. Beaches and the outdoors: The Hague provides both urban attractions and lovely outside scenery. The Hague's Scheveningen, a coastal resort town, is renowned for its pristine beaches, lively promenade, and exciting nightlife. Visitors may walk along the vibrant Scheveningen Pier, unwind in beach clubs, or participate in beach activities. The surrounding Scheveningse Bosjes and Westduinpark provide places for leisurely walks and picnics.

4. The Hague's vibrant cultural scene is home to various museums, art galleries, and theaters. A vast collection of contemporary artwork, including pieces by Mondrian and Picasso, is on display in the Gemeentemuseum Den Haag. The legendary graphic designer M.C. Escher's mind-bending creations are displayed at the Escher Museum. The city also holds many festivals, concerts, and cultural activities yearly.

5. Gardens and Parks: The Hague is renowned for its lush landscaping and immaculate parks. Beautiful floral displays may be found at the lovely Westbroekpark, especially during the International Fireworks Festival. The Haagse Bos historical woods offers a tranquil getaway for those who enjoy the outdoors.

The Hague attracts tourists because of its unique combination of political importance, historical sites, cultural attractions, and scenic beauty. The Hague provides a distinctive and educational experience, regardless of your interests in history, art, international politics, or simply relaxing on the beach.

Rotterdam

Rotterdam, a thriving and international city in the Netherlands, is renowned for its cutting-edge urban planning, bustling port, and contemporary architecture. Rotterdam, the second-largest city in the nation and the capital of the province of South Holland is a vibrant center for commerce, culture, and innovation.

The skyline of Rotterdam, which is lined with historic architectural icons and futuristic buildings, is one of the city's most distinctive characteristics. Structures like the Erasmus Bridge, a spectacular cable-stayed bridge that crosses the River Maas, and the Euromast, an observation tower that provides sweeping city views, show the city's dedication to pushing the frontiers of design and architecture. The Markthal, a colorfully decorated horseshoe-shaped market hall, and the odd Cube Houses, a collection of 45-degree-tilted homes, are two more of Rotterdam's architectural wonders.

Europe's largest port, Rotterdam, is an important logistical and commercial hub. Visitors can observe the astonishing scope of international commerce and nautical activity in the port region, often known as the Maasvlakte. In addition to being a thriving industrial area, the Port of Rotterdam is also a tourist destination in and of itself. Guided boat tours are offered to examine its extensive infrastructure and take in the steady stream of ships worldwide.

DAY 3: East of Amsterdam

You'll find various sights and locations east of Amsterdam, providing Here are a few of the region's highlights:

Museums near Arnhem

The city of Arnhem in the eastern Netherlands has a rich cultural and historical experience. Here are several museums in the area of Arnhem that you might like to visit:

1. The Netherlands Open Air Museum (Nederlands Openluchtmuseum), situated outside of Arnhem, offers a fascinating tour of the nation's history. The museum displays several ages of traditional Dutch architecture, practices, and daily life. Visitors may visit entire buildings, engage with costumed tour guides, and learn about Dutch heritage and culture.

2. Airborne Museum 'Hartenstein': Housed in the old British military headquarters from the Battle of Arnhem in World War II, the Airborne Museum 'Hartenstein' provides a moving and immersive experience. The museum offers a thorough knowledge of the circumstances surrounding Operation Market Garden through its exhibitions, which include first-person accounts, relics, and audiovisual shows.

3. Museum Arnhem: The Museum Arnhem, housed in a beautiful historic structure with views of the Rhine River, specializes in modern and contemporary art. The museum's collection includes Dutch and foreign artists' works from various creative disciplines. Every visit to the museum is a distinctive creative experience since the exhibitions cover a variety of subjects, and the museum also holds temporary displays.

4. Netherlands Water Museum (Nederlands Water Museum): The Netherlands Water Museum, located close to Arnhem, offers information on the significance of water management and the nation's relationship with water. Through interactive exhibitions, visitors may learn about water conservation, flood avoidance, and the world's water concerns. The museum offers visitors of all ages a fun and instructive experience.

5. Het Nationale Park De Hoge Veluwe: This large national park, which is not a museum in the classic sense, is home to the Kröller-Müller Museum. This well-known museum houses a sizable

collection of contemporary artwork, which includes pieces by Vincent van Gogh. The park's stunning natural environs, which include forests, heaths, and dunes, are also open to exploration by visitors.

The experiences available at these museums close to Arnhem are varied, ranging from studying Dutch history and culture to examining contemporary art and environmental concerns. These museums offer interesting and captivating experiences for visitors interested in learning about World War II history, appreciating art, or obtaining knowledge about water management.

Utrecht

Utrecht, a fascinating and ancient city in the center of the Netherlands, charms tourists with its attractive canals, medieval architecture, and lively cultural scene. Utrecht, one of the nation's oldest cities, has a long and illustrious history of over 2,000 years.

1. The Dom Tower, the highest church tower in the Netherlands, is located in the center of Utrecht. A beautiful perspective of the city and its surroundings may be obtained by ascending to the top of the Dom Tower. With outdoor cafés, street performers, and a buzzing atmosphere, the Domplein, the square surrounding the tower, is likewise a hive of activity.

2. The Oudegracht and Nieuwegracht canals in Utrecht add to the city's charm. Quaint cafés, eateries, and distinctive shops surround these waterways. Exploring the city's historic core on a boat trip

or simply wandering around the canals is a great way to experience it.

3. The city has a thriving cultural scene, with several theaters, galleries, and museums. One of the highlights is the Centraal Museum, located in a former medieval monastery and features a varied collection of artwork and historical relics, including pieces by Dutch artists like Rietveld and Van Scorel. The self-playing musical instrument-focused Museum Speelklok delivers a fun and engaging experience.

Chapter 07
THE NETHERLANDS

A trip to the Netherlands offers the chance to explore its illustrious past, dynamic culture, and breathtaking natural beauty. This charming little nation in Northwestern Europe has various tourist sites and activities to suit all visitors.

Exploring Amsterdam, the renowned capital of the Netherlands, is one of the attractions of a trip there. Amsterdam is a city that skillfully combines the old with the contemporary. It is well known for its scenic canals, lovely narrow homes, and top-notch museums. Wandering through the famed Jordaan neighborhood, touring the Rijksmuseum and Van Gogh Museum, or enjoying a leisurely boat ride around the city's canals are all tourist options.

The Netherlands has many more cities worth seeing in addition to Amsterdam. The contemporary architecture and thriving cultural life of Rotterdam provide a sharp contrast to the old-world appeal of Amsterdam. The Hague, the nation's political epicenter, is home to influential organizations like the International Court of Justice and the Mauritshuis Museum, which houses works of art, including Vermeer's "Girl with a Pearl Earring."

The Netherlands cannot be discussed without mentioning its breathtaking countryside. The Dutch landscape is stunning with its recognizable windmills, tulip fields, and charming towns. Millions of people go to Keukenhof, the most extensive flower garden in the world, every year to see the colorful displays of tulips and other springtime blooms. The Kinderdijk windmills, a UNESCO World Heritage monument, also give insight into the nation's earlier conflict with water.

The Netherlands has several national parks and nature reserves for those who like the outdoors. With its extensive heathlands, deep woodlands, and variety of fauna, Hoge Veluwe National Park is a refuge for hikers and bikers. With its system of waterways and wetlands, the Biesbosch National Park is a haven for birdwatchers and boaters.

With a vast network of well-maintained bike trails, the Netherlands is also well known for its riding culture, enabling tourists to explore the nation at leisure. One of the most well-liked activities for tourists is to rent bicycles and go for a leisurely ride through beautiful scenery.

The Dutch are also renowned for being warm and inviting, making guests feel right at home. The nation's cuisine is also interesting to explore; locals like classic Dutch fares like herring, stroopwafels, and bitterballen.

In conclusion, a trip to the Netherlands offers a fascinating fusion of the country's past, present, and future. The Netherlands guarantees a fantastic experience, whether you want to explore the picturesque canals of Amsterdam, marvel at windmills and tulip fields, or immerse yourself in the country's numerous towns and national parks.

Festivals & Holidays

The Netherlands is renowned for its colorful festivals and holidays that offer a chance to participate in the nation's rich cultural traditions. In the Netherlands, the following essential festivals and holidays are observed:

1. King's Day (Koningsdag): King's Day, observed on April 27th, is one of the most eagerly awaited and vibrant occasions in the Netherlands. King Willem Alexander's birthday is commemorated with street celebrations, parades, live music events, and flea markets. People participate in numerous national festivals while wearing orange, the national color.

2. Carnival: A bright and active holiday occurring in the days preceding Lent, Carnival is observed in the southern regions of the Netherlands. Extensive parades, vibrant costumes, music, and dancing bring the streets to life. The Carnival celebrations in places like Maastricht,'s-Hertogenbosch, and Breda are well known.

3. Sinterklaas: On December 5, the Dutch celebrate Sinterklaas or St. Nicholas. It involves the arrival of Sinterklaas and his "Zwarte Pieten" (Black Petes) assistants on a riverboat from Spain. Children get gifts, and parades and other Sinterklaas-related events take place all around the nation.

4. Liberation Day (Bevrijdingsdag): This holiday, observed on May 5, honors the end of the German occupation of the Netherlands

during World War II. Because it is a national holiday, numerous celebrations, concerts, and festivals are held all around the nation to honor those who have given their lives for freedom.

5. Amsterdam Dance Event (ADE): ADE is one of the world's biggest conferences and events for electronic music. Every year in October, it draws DJs, producers, and music lovers worldwide. The festival includes a variety of electronic music genres as well as panel talks, seminars, and performances at different Amsterdam locations.

6. Flower Parade (Bloemencorso): Several flower parades are held in the spring and summer since the Netherlands is well-known for its breathtaking tulip fields. Thousands of onlookers flock to these parades, which include artistically painted floats decked with vibrant flowers. One of the nation's biggest and most well-known flower parades is the Bloemencorso, which takes place in Zundert.

These are a handful of the numerous festivals and holidays observed in the Netherlands. There is always something fascinating going on throughout the year, giving visitors a chance to immerse themselves in the Netherlands' vibrant ambiance and festive spirit, from formal events anchored in Dutch culture to globally famous music festivals.

Books & Films

The Netherlands has a strong literary and cinematic legacy, producing several well-known works that have significantly influenced domestically and abroad. Here are a few lines:

Books:

1. Anne Frank's "The Diary of a Young Girl" is one of history's most well-known and significant books. Anne Frank wrote this famous journal while hiding from the Nazis in Amsterdam. It offers a dramatic first-person narrative of the Holocaust and has stirred meaningful conversations about tolerance and human rights.

2. Herman Koch's "The Dinner" depicts the tale of two spouses who had dinner together to address an unfortunate occurrence involving their teenage kids. As the evening progresses, secrets are revealed, tensions increase, and the complexity of human morals and conduct is revealed.

3. Harry Mulisch's "The Assault" examines the long-lasting effects of a single incident on the life of a man named Anton and is set against the backdrop of World War II. It explores issues like guilt, accountability, and the difficulties associated with memory and identity.

4. "The Hiding Place" by Corrie Ten Boom: This memoir, based on an accurate tale, details Corrie Ten Boom's experiences and those of her family as they put their lives in danger to Jewish shelter refugees during the Nazi occupation. In the face of difficulty, it is a monument to bravery, faith, and the strength of compassion.

Films:

1. "Black Book" (Zwartboek), a critically acclaimed World War II thriller directed by Paul Verhoeven, tells the tale of a Jewish lady

who joins the Dutch resistance after her family is murdered. The movie addresses betrayal, survival, and atonement while filled with mystery, suspense, and moral quandaries.

2. "Turkish Delight" (Turks Fruit) is a well-known Dutch movie adapted from the same-titled novel by Jan Wolkers. Paul Verhoeven directed it. It captures the essence of the Dutch counterculture of the 1970s by narrating the passionate and tumultuous love affair between an artist and a young lady.

3. "Character" (Karakter): This Academy Award-winning film, an adaptation of Ferdinand Bordewijk's novel, examines the turbulent relationship between a driven young man and his controlling father in early 20th-century Rotterdam. The battle for uniqueness, aspiration, and class are all compellingly portrayed.

4. "The Vanishing" (Spoorloos): This psychological suspense film is directed by George Sluizer and centers on the hunt for a lady who inexplicably vanishes while on vacation with her lover. The film is renowned for its eerie atmosphere and challenging conclusion.

By delivering compelling storylines, delving into complex subjects, and reflecting the cultural and historical backdrop of the nation, these books and movies give a window into the rich literary and cinematic environment of the Netherlands.

Climate

The Netherlands has a moderate maritime climate, significantly impacted by its location near the North Sea and the predominate westerly winds. The Dutch environment can be summarized in the following ways:

1. Moderate Winters: The Netherlands experiences mild winters, with average temperatures in the coldest months of December, January, and February hovering between 0°C (32°F) and six °C (43°F). Snowfall happens often, although it rarely covers much ground.

2. Pleasant Summers: The Netherlands has cool, pleasant summers, with average highs in July and August of 20°C (68°F) and 17°C (63°F), respectively. However, during heatwaves, temperatures can occasionally rise to the mid to high 20s°C (77-86°F).

3. Rainfall: The Netherlands has moderate to heavy amounts of precipitation all year, with July and August being the wettest months. Cloudy days are typical, and rain showers are frequently but very briefly present. Generally, the country's eastern portions experience less rainfall than its southern coastal regions.

4. Wind: The Netherlands is renowned for having windy weather, especially along the shore and in the open countryside. The country's predominant westerly winds, which originate in the North Sea, have the potential to be gusty and have an impact on local weather patterns.

5. The Netherlands has four seasons, with spring and autumn being the mildest and most transitional. Springtime ushers in blooming flowers, especially the well-known tulips, while fall displays stunning leaves hues.

It's crucial to remember that weather conditions might change from one year to the next and that catastrophic weather phenomena like storms and torrential rain are probable. The Dutch climate's warm temperatures and plentiful rainfall are significant factors in the country's beautiful green scenery, vivid flora, and high agricultural output.

When planning to travel to the Netherlands, it is wise to consult the local weather forecast because it might affect outdoor activities and sightseeing.

Dutch Helpful Phrases

Here are some helpful Dutch phrases that you can use during your visit to the Netherlands:

1. Hello - Hallo

2. Good morning - Goedemorgen

3. Good afternoon - Goedemiddag

4. Good evening - Goedenavond

5. Goodbye - Tot Ziens

6. Thank you - Dank u (formal) / Dank je (informal)

7. Please - Alstublieft (standard) / Alsjeblieft (informal)

8. Excuse me - Excuse me

9. Sorry - Sorry

10. Yes - Ja

11. No - Nee

12. Do you speak English? - Spreekt u Engels? (formal) / Spreek je Engels? (informal)

13. I don't understand - Ik begrijp het niet

14. Could you help me, please? - Kunt u me alstublieft helpen? (formal) / Kun je me alsjeblieft helpen? (informal)

15. Where is...? - Waar is...?

16. How much does it cost? - Hoeveel kost het?

17. Can I pay by credit card? - Kan ik met creditcard betalen?

18. Can you recommend a good restaurant? - Kunt u een goed restaurant aanbevelen? (formal) / Kun je een goed restaurant aanbevelen? (informal)

19. Cheers! - Proost!

20. Have a nice day! - Fijne dag!

These phrases should be helpful for basic communication and interactions during your time in the Netherlands. Many Dutch people also speak English, so if you encounter any language barriers, don't hesitate to ask if someone can communicate in English. Dutch people generally appreciate the effort to learn a few phrases in their language, so don't be afraid to try it!

Conclusion

We hope you have enjoyed reading through the pages of our travel guide and are now motivated and ready to start planning your trip to Amsterdam and the Netherlands. This location offers a rich tapestry of experiences that will leave a lasting impact, from the energetic streets of Amsterdam to the scenic countryside and lovely villages.

We have given you insightful information, helpful advice, and suggestions to help you plan an unforgettable vacation throughout this book. You'll find the information you need to make the most of your holiday, whether you're interested in discovering the cultural gems of Amsterdam, taking enthralling day excursions to nearby cities, or getting a true sense of the distinctive Dutch way of life.

The appeal of Amsterdam resides in its contrast between old-world beauty and modern energy. There are countless options for exploration and discovery thanks to its network of canals, attractive districts, and top-notch museums. You will genuinely understand Amsterdam's soul by meandering through the city's streets, enjoying regional cuisine, and immersing yourself in its rich cultural legacy.

However, the voyage doesn't finish there by itself. With its breathtaking scenery, fascinating historic sites, and welcoming citizens, the Netherlands is a nation of surprises. By stepping beyond the capital city, you may discover unique experiences and hidden jewels in the towns like Haarlem, Delft, and Utrecht. Each place has its distinct appeal, from the vibrant tulip fields to the architectural wonders of Rotterdam and The Hague.

Be sure to adopt the Dutch way of life while you travel across the Netherlands. Get on a bike and ride across the countryside and cities like a local. Talk to the welcoming folks, enjoy the delectable Dutch food, and get to know the rich heritage and culture that make this nation unique.

We hope this guide will give you the confidence to design your unique journey based on your interests and choices. The Netherlands has plenty to offer everyone, whether you are good in art, history, or nature or seeking new experiences.

Take on a sense of inquiry, openness, and appreciation for the beauty in your surroundings as you embark on your voyage. Allow yourself to become lost in Amsterdam's winding alleyways, be mesmerized by the countryside's windmills, and make lifelong memories.

Best wishes for a fantastic trip in Amsterdam and the Netherlands are extended. As you immerse yourself in the rich tapestry of Dutch culture and history, may your travels be full of awe-inspiring experiences, meaningful relationships, and a feeling of wonder. Congratulations, and have fun on your fantastic journey.